Modern Critical Interpretations

Tennessee Williams's
A Streetcar Named Desire

Modern Critical Interpretations

The Oresteia
Beowulf
The General Prologue to
  The Canterbury Tales
The Pardoner's Tale
The Knight's Tale
The Divine Comedy
Exodus
Genesis
The Gospels
The Iliad
The Book of Job
Volpone
Doctor Faustus
The Revelation of St.
  John the Divine
The Song of Songs
Oedipus Rex
The Aeneid
The Duchess of Malfi
Antony and Cleopatra
As You Like It
Coriolanus
Hamlet
Henry IV, Part I
Henry IV, Part II
Henry V
Julius Caesar
King Lear
Macbeth
Measure for Measure
The Merchant of Venice
A Midsummer Night's
  Dream
Much Ado About
  Nothing
Othello
Richard II
Richard III
The Sonnets
Taming of the Shrew
The Tempest
Twelfth Night
The Winter's Tale
Emma
Mansfield Park
Pride and Prejudice
The Life of Samuel
  Johnson
Moll Flanders
Robinson Crusoe
Tom Jones
The Beggar's Opera
Gray's Elegy
Paradise Lost
The Rape of the Lock
Tristram Shandy
Gulliver's Travels

Evelina
The Marriage of Heaven
  and Hell
Songs of Innocence and
  Experience
Jane Eyre
Wuthering Heights
Don Juan
The Rime of the Ancient
  Mariner
Bleak House
David Copperfield
Hard Times
A Tale of Two Cities
Middlemarch
The Mill on the Floss
Jude the Obscure
The Mayor of
  Casterbridge
The Return of the Native
Tess of the D'Urbervilles
The Odes of Keats
Frankenstein
Vanity Fair
Barchester Towers
The Prelude
The Red Badge of
  Courage
The Scarlet Letter
The Ambassadors
Daisy Miller, The Turn
  of the Screw, and
  Other Tales
The Portrait of a Lady
Billy Budd, Benito Cer-
  eno, Bartleby the Scriv-
  ener, and Other Tales
Moby-Dick
The Tales of Poe
Walden
Adventures of
  Huckleberry Finn
The Life of Frederick
  Douglass
Heart of Darkness
Lord Jim
Nostromo
A Passage to India
Dubliners
A Portrait of the Artist as
  a Young Man
Ulysses
Kim
The Rainbow
Sons and Lovers
Women in Love
1984
Major Barbara

Man and Superman
Pygmalion
St. Joan
The Playboy of the
  Western World
The Importance of Being
  Earnest
Mrs. Dalloway
To the Lighthouse
My Antonia
An American Tragedy
Murder in the Cathedral
The Waste Land
Absalom, Absalom!
Light in August
Sanctuary
The Sound and the Fury
The Great Gatsby
A Farewell to Arms
The Sun Also Rises
Arrowsmith
Lolita
The Iceman Cometh
Long Day's Journey Into
  Night
The Grapes of Wrath
Miss Lonelyhearts
The Glass Menagerie
A Streetcar Named
  Desire
Their Eyes Were
  Watching God
Native Son
Waiting for Godot
Herzog
All My Sons
Death of a Salesman
Gravity's Rainbow
All the King's Men
The Left Hand of
  Darkness
The Brothers Karamazov
Crime and Punishment
Madame Bovary
The Interpretation of
  Dreams
The Castle
The Metamorphosis
The Trial
Man's Fate
The Magic Mountain
Montaigne's Essays
Remembrance of Things
  Past
The Red and the Black
Anna Karenina
War and Peace

These and other titles in preparation

Modern Critical Interpretations

Tennessee Williams's
A Streetcar Named Desire

Edited and with an introduction by
Harold Bloom
Sterling Professor of the Humanities
Yale University

Chelsea House Publishers ◊ *1988*
NEW YORK ◊ NEW HAVEN ◊ PHILADELPHIA

© 1988 by Chelsea House Publishers, a division of Chelsea
House Educational Communications, Inc.,
  95 Madison Avenue, New York, NY 10016
  345 Whitney Avenue, New Haven, CT 06511
  5068B West Chester Pike, Edgemont, PA 19028

Introduction © 1988 by Harold Bloom

Printed and bound in the United States of America

10 9 8 7 6 5 4 3 2 1

∞ The paper used in this publication meets the minimum
requirements of the American National Standard for
Permanence of Paper for Printed Library Materials,
Z39.48–1984.

Library of Congress Cataloging-in-Publication Data
Tennessee Williams's A streetcar named Desire.
  (Modern critical interpretations)
  Bibliography: p.
  Includes index.
  1. Williams, Tennessee, 1911–   . Streetcar named
Desire.   I. Bloom, Harold.   II. Series.
PS3545.I5365S8275 1988   812'.54   87–11626
ISBN 1–55546–045–3 (alk. paper)

Contents

Editor's Note / vii

Introduction / 1
    HAROLD BLOOM

America's New Culture Hero:
Feelings without Words / 7
    ROBERT BRUSTEIN

Truth and Dramatic Mode in
A Streetcar Named Desire / 17
    ALVIN B. KERNAN

A Streetcar Named Desire—Nietzsche Descending / 21
    JOSEPH N. RIDDEL

The Tragic Downfall of Blanche DuBois / 33
    LEONARD BERKMAN

Tennessee Williams: Streetcar to Glory / 41
    C. W. E. BIGSBY

Realism and Theatricalism in
A Streetcar Named Desire / 49
    MARY ANN CORRIGAN

The Cards Indicate a Voyage on
A Streetcar Named Desire / 61
    LEONARD QUIRINO

Drama of Intimacy and Tragedy of Incomprehension:
A Streetcar Named Desire Reconsidered / 79
    BERT CARDULLO

From "Tarantula Arms" to "Della Robbia Blue": The
Tennessee Williams Tragicomic Transit Authority / 93
    JOHN M. RODERICK

Madonna at the Poker Night: Pictorial Elements in
Tennessee Williams's *A Streetcar Named Desire* / 103
    HENRY I. SCHVEY

The Fate of the Symbolic in *A Streetcar Named
Desire* / 111
    KATHLEEN HULLEY

Chronology / 123

Contributors / 127

Bibliography / 129

Acknowledgments / 131

Index / 133

Editor's Note

This book brings together a representative selection of the best criticism available upon *A Streetcar Named Desire,* the major drama by Tennessee Williams. The critical essays are reprinted here in the chronological order of their original publication. I am grateful to Daniel Klotz for his work as a researcher on this volume.

My introduction considers Williams as a dramatic lyricist in the manner of Hart Crane, rather than as a lyrical dramatist in the wake of Chekhov, and then offers an exegesis of *Streetcar* in which Blanche is judged to be a not wholly adequate emblem of Williams's vision of himself as a continuator of Crane and Rimbaud.

Robert Brustein begins the chronological sequence with his shrewd account of *Streetcar*'s Stanley Kowalski (as played by the young Marlon Brando) as the archetype of a particular kind of popular culture hero in America, a figure of inarticulate pathos. In a brief but cogent study, Alvin B. Kernan contrasts the "realistic" (Stanley) and "romantic" (Blanche) visions in *Streetcar*. In Joseph N. Riddel's analysis of the play, we are offered a Nietzschean critique of Williams's failure to qualify his realism in the interests of a more Dionysian perspective upon Blanche.

Leonard Berkman views Blanche's downfall as an instance of tragic irony, a judgment somewhat at variance with that of C. W. E. Bigsby, for whom Blanche's fate illustrates the desperation of Williams's American Romanticism. Perhaps these conflicts of interpretation are partly resolved in Mary Ann Corrigan's reading, which praises *Streetcar* for reconciling those stage rivals, realism and theatricalism.

In an essay on the play's symbolism, Leonard Quirino centers upon two images: the cards of destiny and the voyage of experience. For Bert Cardullo, *Streetcar* is a domestic tragedy that dramatizes modes of intimacy that lack all comprehension. Tragicomedy, a rather different genre, is invoked by John M. Roderick as the proper context for judging Williams's achievement in the play.

Henry I. Schvey concentrates upon *Streetcar*'s visual effects, which convince him that the drama's design is one of purification through purgatorial suffering. In this book's final essay, Kathleen Hulley deconstructs *Streetcar* to show the role of our ambivalent social law in Williams's dark representation of the death of desire.

Introduction

I

It is a sad and inexplicable truth that the United States, a dramatic nation, continues to have so limited a literary achievement in the drama. American literature, from Emerson to the present moment, is a distinguished tradition. The poetry of Whitman, Dickinson, Frost, Stevens, Eliot, W. C. Williams, Hart Crane, R. P. Warren, Elizabeth Bishop down through the generation of my own contemporaries—John Ashbery, James Merrill, A. R. Ammons, and others—has an unquestionable eminence, and takes a vital place in Western literature. Prose fiction from Hawthorne and Melville on through Mark Twain and Henry James to Cather and Dreiser, Faulkner, Hemingway, Fitzgerald, Nathanael West, and Pynchon, has almost a parallel importance. The line of essayists and critics from Emerson and Thoreau to Kenneth Burke and beyond constitutes another crucial strand of our national letters. But where is the American drama in comparison to all this, and in relation to the long cavalcade of western drama from Aeschylus to Beckett?

The American theater, by the common estimate of its most eminent critics, touches an initial strength with Eugene O'Neill, and then proceeds to the more varied excellences of Thornton Wilder, Tennessee Williams, Arthur Miller, Edward Albee, and Sam Shepard. That sequence is clearly problematical, and becomes even more worrisome when we move from playwrights to plays. Which are our dramatic works that matter most? *Long Day's Journey Into Night,* certainly; perhaps *The Iceman Cometh;* evidently *A Streetcar Named Desire* and *Death of a Salesman;* perhaps again *The Skin of Our Teeth* and *The Zoo Story*—it is not God's plenty. And I will venture the speculation that our drama palpably is not yet literary enough. By this I do not just mean that O'Neill writes very badly, or Miller very baldly; they do, but so did Dreiser, and *Sister Carrie* and *An American Tragedy* prevail nevertheless. Nor do I wish to be an American Matthew Ar-

1

nold (whom I loathe above all other critics) and proclaim that our dramatists simply have not known enough. They know more than enough, and that is part of the trouble.

Literary tradition, as I have come to understand it, masks the agon between past and present as a benign relationship, whether personal or societal. The actual transferences between the force of the literary past and the potential of writing in the present tend to be darker, even if they do not always or altogether follow the defensive patterns of what Sigmund Freud called "family romances." Whether or not an ambivalence, however repressed, towards the past's force is felt by the new writer and is manifested in his work seems to depend entirely upon the ambition and power of the oncoming artist. If he aspires after strength, and can attain it, then he must struggle with both a positive and a negative transference, false connections because necessarily imagined ones, between a composite precursor and himself. His principal resource in that agon will be his own native gift for interpretation, or as I am inclined to call it, strong misreading. Revising his precursor, he will create himself, make himself into a kind of changeling, and so he will become, in an illusory but highly pragmatic way, his own father.

The most literary of our major dramatists, and clearly I mean "literary" in a precisely descriptive sense, neither pejorative nor eulogistic, was Tennessee Williams. Wilder, with his intimate connections to *Finnegans Wake* and Gertrude Stein, might seem to dispute this placement, and Wilder was certainly more literate than Williams. But Wilder had a benign relation to his crucial precursor, Joyce, and did not aspire after a destructive strength. Williams did, and suffered the fate he prophesied and desired; the strength destroyed his later work, and his later life, and thus joined itself to the American tradition of self-destructive genius. Williams truly had one precursor only: Hart Crane, the greatest of our lyrical poets, after Whitman and Dickinson, and the most self-destructive figure in our national literature, surpassing all others in this, as in so many regards.

Williams asserted he had other precursors also: D. H. Lawrence, and Chekhov in the drama. These were outward influences, and benefited Williams well enough, but they were essentially formal, and so not the personal and societal family romance of authentic poetic influence. Hart Crane made Williams into more of a dramatic lyrist, though writing in prose, than the lyrical dramatist that Williams is supposed to have been. Though this influence—perhaps more nearly an identification—helped form *The Glass Menagerie* and (less overtly) *A Streetcar Named Desire,* and in a lesser mode *Summer and Smoke* and *Suddenly Last Summer,* it also led to such disasters of misplaced lyricism as the dreadful *Camino Real* and the dreary *The Night of the Iguana*. (*Cat on a Hot Tin Roof,* one of Williams's best plays, does not seem to me to show any influence of Crane.) Williams's long aesthetic decline covered thirty years, from 1953 to 1983, and reflected the sorrows of a seer who, by his early forties, had outlived his own vision. Hart Crane, self-slain at thirty-two, had set for Williams a High Romantic paradigm that helped cause Williams, his heart as dry as summer dust, to burn to the socket.

II

The epigraph to *A Streetcar Named Desire* is a quatrain from Hart Crane's "The Broken Tower," the poet's elegy for his gift, his vocation, his life, and so Crane's precise equivalent of Shelley's *Triumph of Life,* Keat's *Fall of Hyperion,* and Whitman's "When Lilacs Last in the Dooryard Bloom'd." Tennessee Williams, in his long thirty years of decline after composing *A Streetcar Named Desire,* had no highly designed, powerfully executed elegy for his own poetic self. Unlike Crane, his American Romantic precursor and aesthetic paradigm, Williams had to live out the slow degradation of the waning of his potential, and so endured the triumph of life over his imagination.

Streetcar sustains a first rereading, after thirty years away from it, more strongly than I had expected. It is, inevitably, more remarkable on the stage than in the study, but the fusion of Williams's lyrical and dramatic talents in it has prevailed over time, at least so far. The play's flaws, in performance, ensue from its implicit tendency to sensationalize its characters, Blanche DuBois in particular. Directors and actresses have made such sensationalizing altogether explicit, with the sad result prophesied by Kenneth Tynan twenty-five years ago. The playgoer forgets that Blanche's only strengths are "nostalgia and hope," that she is "the desperate exceptional woman," and that her fall is a parable, rather than an isolated squalor:

> When, finally, she is removed to the mental home, we should feel that a part of civilization is going with her. Where ancient drama teaches us to reach nobility by contemplation of what is noble, modern American drama conjures us to contemplate what might have been noble, but is now humiliated, ignoble in the sight of all but the compassionate.

Tynan, though accurate enough, still might have modified the image of Blanche taking a part of civilization away with her into madness. Though Blanche yearns for the values of the aesthetic, she scarcely embodies them, being in this failure a masochistic self-parody on the part of Williams himself. His *Memoirs* portray Williams incessantly in the role of Blanche, studying the nostalgias, and inching along the wavering line between hope and paranoia. Williams, rather than Blanche, sustains Tynan's analysis of the lost nobility, now humiliated, that American drama conjures us to contemplate.

The fall of Blanche is a parable, not of American civilization's lost nobility, but of the failure of the American literary imagination to rise above its recent myths of recurrent defeat. Emerson admonished us, his descendants, to go beyond the Great Defeat of the Crucifixion and to demand Victory instead, a victory of the senses as well as of the soul. Walt Whitman, taking up Emerson's challenge directly, set the heroic pattern so desperately emulated by Hart Crane, and which is then repeated in a coarser tone in Williams's life and work.

It must seem curious, at first, to regard Blanche DuBois as a failed Whitmanian, but essentially that is her aesthetic identity. Confronted by the revelation of her young husband's preference for an older man over herself, Blanche falls downwards and outwards into nymphomania, phantasmagoric hopes, pseudo-imaginative collages of memory and desire. Her Orphic, psychic rending by the amiably brutal Stanley Kowalski, a rough but effective version of D. H. Lawrence's vitalistic vision of male force, is pathetic rather than tragic, not because Stanley necessarily is mindless, but because she unnecessarily has made herself mindless, by failing the pragmatic test of experience.

Williams's most effective blend of lyrical vision and dramatic irony in the play comes in the agony of Blanche's cry against Stanley to Stella, his wife and her sister:

> He acts like an animal, has an animal's habits! Eats like one, moves like one, talks like one! There's even something—sub-human—something not quite to the stage of humanity yet! Yes, something—ape-like about him, like one of those pictures I've seen in—anthropological studies! Thousands and thousands of years have passed him right by, and there he is—Stanley Kowalski—survivor of the stone age! Bearing the raw meat home from the kill in the jungle! And you—*you* here—*waiting* for him! Maybe he'll strike you or maybe grunt and kiss you! That is, if kisses have been discovered yet! Night falls and the other

apes gather! There in the front of the cave, all grunting like him, and swilling and gnawing and hulking! His poker night!—you call it—this party of apes! Somebody growls—some creature snatches at something—the fight is on! *God!* Maybe we are a long way from being made in God's image, but Stella—my sister—there has been *some* progress since then! Such things as art—as poetry and music—such kinds of new light have come into the world since then! In some kinds of people some tenderer feelings have had some little beginning! That we have got to make *grow!* And *cling* to, and hold as our flag! In this dark march toward whatever it is we're approaching. . . . *Don't—don't hang back with the brutes!*

The lyricism here takes its strength from the ambivalence of what at once attracts and dismays both Blanche and Williams. Dramatic irony, terrible in its antithetical pathos, results here from Blanche's involuntary self-condemnation, since she herself has hung back with the brutes while merely blinking at the new light of the aesthetic. Stanley, being what he is, is clearly less to blame than Blanche, who was capable of more but failed in will.

Williams, in his *Memoirs*, haunted as always by Hart Crane, refers to his precursor as "a tremendous and yet fragile artist," and then associates both himself and Blanche with the fate of Crane, a suicide by drowning in the Caribbean:

I am as much of an hysteric as . . . Blanche; a codicil to my will provides for the disposition of my body in this way. "Sewn up in a clean white sack and dropped over board, twelve hours north of Havana, so that my bones may rest not too far from those of Hart Crane . . ."

At the conclusion of *Memoirs*, Williams again associated Crane both with his own vocation and his own limitations, following Crane even in an identification with the young Rimbaud:

A poet such as the young Rimbaud is the only writer of whom I can think, at this moment, who could escape from words into the sensations of being, through his youth, turbulent with revolution, permitted articulation by nights of absinthe. And of course there is Hart Crane. Both of these poets touched fire that burned them alive. And perhaps it is only through self-immolation of such a nature that we living beings can offer to you the entire truth of ourselves within the reasonable boundaries of a book.

It is the limitation of *Memoirs*, and in some sense even of *A Streetcar Named Desire*, that we cannot accept either Williams or poor Blanche as a Rimbaud or a Hart Crane. Blanche cannot be said to have touched fire that burned her alive. Yet Williams earns the relevance of the play's great epigraph to Blanche's terrible fate:

> And so it was I entered the broken world
> To trace the visionary company of love, its voice
> An instant in the wind (I know not whither hurled)
> But not for long to hold each desperate choice.

America's New Culture Hero: Feelings without Words

Robert Brustein

In the last eight or ten years Americans have been charmed by a new culture hero, with far-reaching effects upon the quality of our spoken arts. In a persistent effort to find a voice for America, to find a language, vocabulary, and intonation peculiarly our own, we have come temporarily to settle for no voice at all. The stage, motion pictures, television, and even popular music are now exalting an inarticulate hero, who—for all the dependence of these media on language—cannot talk.

Of medium height and usually of lower-class birth, his most familiar physical characteristic is his surly and discontented expression. His eyes peer out at the world from under beetling brows; his uncombed hair falls carelessly over his forehead; his right hand rests casually on his right hip. He is extremely muscular and walks with a slouching, shuffling gait. He scratches himself often, slumps in chairs, and almost never smiles. He is also identified by the sounds which issue from his mouth. He squeezes, he grunts, he passes his hand over his eyes and forehead, he stares steadily, he turns away, he scratches, then again faces his adversary, and finally speaks. What he says is rarely important but he has mesmerized his auditor by the effort he takes to say it. He has communicated not information but feeling; he has revealed an inner life of unspecified anguish and torment.

From this description it should be clear that I am talking about a character familiar not through any particular work of art but rather through association with the many actors who impersonate it—Marlon Brando, James Dean, Paul Newman, Ben Gazzara, John Cassevetes, Montgomery

---

From *Commentary* 25, no. 2 (February 1958). © 1958 by Robert Brustein.

Clift, and the countless others whose identification with sex, violence, and incoherency unites them as a school. What endears this peculiar creature to the general public? Where does he come from, what is his significance, and what has been his effect on present-day dramatic writing?

The inarticulate hero of today clearly finds his immediate origin in Tennessee Williams's Stanley Kowalski as interpreted by Marlon Brando. His tradition, however, goes further back than *A Streetcar Named Desire*. Ever since Eugene O'Neill created Yank in *The Hairy Ape* (1922), American playwrights have been trying to find dramatic expression for the man of lower birth—of northern urban or southern rural origin—who was denied the language and manners of his more cultured countrymen. Quite often, in spite of superior physical strength, this man was pictured as a victim. O'Neill's stoker Yank has the power to make the ship go, but once on land, in the clutch of the cold concrete city, he is overcome by pushing crowds, political complexity, and the ridicule of a high-born woman, and finally is crushed to death while trying to embrace an ape, the only animal with whom he finds intellectual communion. The sharecroppers, migrant workers, and tramps of John Steinbeck are victims too, but since his heroes are more unqualifiedly noble than Yank (for Steinbeck virtue and poverty are almost always equated) their defeat is political rather than personal and implies an indictment of society. In the early works of Clifford Odets, the political note is struck even harder. O'Neill's and Steinbeck's proletarian heroes are often characterized by their lack of verbal coherence, but Odets's heroes are singular for their extreme verbosity. Rather than being speechless in the face of their dilemma, they never stop talking about it.

The unspoken assumption of the Group Theatre, the repertory company that produced most of the proletarian dramas of the 1930s, was that sensitivity, fire, intensity, and sexual potency were primarily the properties of the underprivileged and the uneducated. Using the acting techniques of Stanislavsky in forms altered to suit American needs, the Group Theatre created a style with which to import the supercharged mood of these plays and an acting company to impersonate the underprivileged heroes. The most representative actors in this company, John Garfield and Luther Adler, rather than being stammerers, were highly articulate; rather than being enmeshed in a world too complex for their intelligence, they were extremely precise about the forces leading them to ruin.

The Group Theatre was dissolved in the early 1940s, but some of its functions were taken over by the Actors Studio, organized in the late 1940s by former members. Unlike the Group Theatre, the Actors Studio was designed not as a production unit but primarily as a workshop where actors could perfect their craft. And yet, because of the widely publicized popular success of some of its members, the Actors Studio has managed to wield more influence on acting styles and playwrighting material than any other single organization, even those dedicated to the actual production of plays. It is in the Actors Studio that most of today's proletarian heroes are being spawned.

Although much (if not all) of the acting that emerges from the Actors Studio would seem to indicate that the proletarian is still considered more interesting, more electric, and capable of deeper feelings than the owner of a store or the manager of a bank, this assumption seems no longer accompanied by a political conviction. The proletarian hero of the 1950s has lost his political flavor and even more important, his power of speech. He combines the inarticulacy of the Hairy Ape with the dynamism (now adjusted from a boil to a simmer) of the Odets hero, and adds to these certain qualities which neither Odets nor O'Neill had endowed him with. Stanley Kowalski is the first character in American drama to unite most of the identifying characteristics of this hero, but it is difficult to determine how much actor Marlon Brando and director Elia Kazan, both Actors Studio associates at the time or soon after, contributed to his formation. All drama is a collaboration, and dramatists find their characters subtly changing coloration in the playing. Stanley Kowalski, as he became known to the general public in the original New York production and the excellent movie made from it, was probably the collaborative product of Williams, Brando, and Kazan. Stanley, as *written* by Williams, is a highly complex and ambiguous character, one who can be taken either as hero or as villain. As a social or cultural figure, Stanley is a villain, in mindless opposition to civilization and culture—the "new man" of the modern world whom Williams seems to find responsible for the present-day decline in art, language, decorum, and culture. As a psychological or sexual figure, however, Stanley exists on a somewhat more heroic moral plane. He is akin to those silent, sullen gamekeepers and grooms of D. H. Lawrence (an early influence on Williams) whose sexuality, though violent, is unmental, unspiritual, and, therefore, in some way free from taint. The conflict between Blanche and Stanley allegorizes the struggle between effeminate culture and masculine libido. It is no accident that Stanley, in the climax of the play, subdues Blanche by a brutal sexual assault. One assumption of the play is plain: culture and tradition are desirable, but breed effeteness and perversity (Blanche is a nymphomaniac) and make one an easy prey to the unenlightened.

It should be clear, even from this brief analysis, that with Stanley,

Williams wrought significant changes in the proletarian hero. If one sympathizes with Stanley it is not because he is underprivileged or exploited or victimized—Stanley is at all times an active character, one who manipulates each situation in which he appears. Rather than expressing dissatisfaction with the grubby conditions in which he lives, he exults in them, and he does not indicate any desire to better himself. More important, Stanley, as brute force incarnate, has no poetry or sensitivity or nobility in him—neither John Garfield nor Luther Adler could ever have played this role. His intelligence is mostly animal cunning and his power of speech limited to expressing basic desires.

And yet, if Williams created an ignoble rather than a noble savage, how do we explain the spectacular success of Brando and the extensive influence his playing of Stanley has had on acting ever since? The answer, I think, lies in the personal values Brando contributed to the role. As played by Brando, Stanley Kowalski somehow emerged as a more appealing, a more sympathetic, and (most important) a more sensitive character than Williams created, and the play became a conflict between two protagonists, one less noble but no less interesting than the other. When Anthony Quinn, taking over the part, played it more like the thick-headed antagonist Williams intended, the focus of the play shifted back to Blanche. There is irony in the fact that, although *Streetcar* is Blanche's tragedy, the villain of the piece became the prototype for a hero, the inarticulate hero of popular culture. After Stanley, the brutal proletarian was rarely to be seen again. As he emerged from the Actors Studio and the pens of the writers who began creating parts for these actors, he had once again acquired a helpless attitude in a hostile world. And although he inherited Stanley Kowalski's speechlessness, his animality, and his violent behavior, these qualities were now seen as marks of profundity of character.

Thus in a period of prosperity and political conformity, the proletarian hero has managed, paradoxically, to accomplish something he failed to do in a period of depression and political radicalism—he has made the audience take notice of him. At a time when America has the largest middle-class population in the world (when, in one sense, it sees itself as entirely middle class), one of its most conspicuous dramatic heroes is poor and uneducated. Although the Broadway audience is predominantly from the cultured, leisured classes, the typical Broadway product (not imported from England or Europe) is peopled with dock workers, drug addicts, juvenile delinquents, prostitutes, pimps, butchers, southern farmers, seamen, machine shop workers, and drifters. By finding "reality" and "truth" (though not necessarily virtue) in the outcasts of society, play-wrights have created a problem they did not have to face in the 1930s: they have estranged their audience from the difficulties of their heroes. I do not wish to repeat the charges made against realism in the drama; its smallness of vision, its prosaicness, and its pedantic re-creation of the least penetrat-ing aspects of life have become all too apparent. I do want to add, how-ever, that when the drama centers on the proletarian and faithfully records his speech, it often becomes mindless, almost anti-intellectual. Ideas and subtle emotions are communicated primarily through speech and even the bluntest emotion loses its meaning if it is not reflected upon. How empty would be the suffering of Lear or Oedipus were it not followed by an illu-mination of the heart and the mind. In limiting the expression of their he-roes, playwrights have limited their heroes' understanding of their suffer-ing. The difficulties of the modern proletarian hero end on an unresolved question—Why?

That the tongue-tied emotionalism of many modern plays is partly the result of directing and acting techniques is indicated by the fact that even in relatively literate plays, inarticulacy is sometimes imposed by the production. In the recent Broadway showing of *Compulsion,* for example, the two actors called upon to play boys of superior mental capacities and wealthy backgrounds brought the same verbal hesitation to their roles they might have used in playing a couple of hoodlums. Broadway apparently has still not devised a technique to communicate intelligence. The paradox of the estranged audience applies to acting as well: although the Broadway audience is relatively coherent and literate, the emphasis on our stage has fallen off the spoken word. The actor uses language only as a secondary instrument. His main purpose is to convey the mute feelings within his soul. The effect is admittedly quite explosive. The struggle within an inco-herent individual trying to express his feelings can be extremely powerful, for one often has the sense that the character's stammers, mumbles, and grunts will, like those of Billy Budd, erupt into violence if they continue to frustrate speech. (Much of O'Neill's power as a playwright stems from his inability to say precisely what he means and his tortuous way of talk-ing round and round a subject.) The consequence of this style of acting, however, is that we presently have an actor's theater. The actor has taken precedence over the playwright; the play has receded before the perfor-mance. One becomes more conscious of the personal problems of the ac-tor than of the character he is playing; in some cases, the actor's and the character's problems become inextricably confused.

The general uninterest in the classics demonstrated by many of today's actors and directors (a recent Equity symposium had the title "The Classics: Are They Avant-Garde?") is closely related to this problem, for most of the classics of dramatic literature depend to a large extent on words. It is significant that one of America's most able theater and movie directors, Elia Kazan, has only directed contemporary works. When asked if he would ever produce Shakespeare, he replied (albeit in all humility), "I never have and I never will. I am interested in the life that is around me. . . ." This is an extraordinary statement, all the more so because so few people in the theater consider it extraordinary. Apart from the intimation that contemporary playwrights probe more deeply into "the life around me" than Shakespeare (or is Kazan concerned only with environmental truth?), these words yield very interesting considerations. Imagine the conductor of the Philharmonic refusing to interpret Mozart and Beethoven on the same grounds. Considering the appalling ignorance most actors have of the works in their field, try to imagine even the most benighted tenor, violinist, or ballerina in a similar state of ignorance. One would look in vain for the same paucity of classical works on the musical, ballet, or operatic stage as one finds on Broadway. In refusing Ibsen, Strindberg, and Yeats a hearing, the interpreters of the drama have usurped the prerogatives of the creative artist, one of whose permissible functions is to be in revolt against the techniques of the past.

Mr. Kazan goes on to express his admiration for Chekhov (the one classical writer known and cherished by most members of the Actors Studio) and this gives us a clue why traditional drama holds no fascination for him. Although Chekhov was a master of language (the language, be it remembered, of the cultured, leisured classes), it is not always the word that communicates his meaning. More often, the action is revealed slowly in fragments of discourse, and seemingly commonplace statements conceal the intense desires and anguish of the characters. Chekhov thus offers relative liberation to the actor and director; he offers a freedom of interpretation not granted by Shakespeare or Shaw. The indirect techniques of Stanislavsky become a possible method of conveying Chekhov's fragments and impressions (although Chekhov complained most of his life that Stanislavsky had misinterpreted his plays) because the subtext, or the feeling behind the word, has gained more importance than the word itself. In less impressionistic plays than Chekhov's, however, the subtext can be a stratagem by which the actor ignores the playwright's meaning, substituting the *feeling* he himself finds to be more compelling. The actor becomes a creator rather than an interpreter, seeking the clue to his performance in his own experience instead of in the experience of the character he is supposed to be playing.

Granted the power of a school of acting and production techniques to impose a special kind of theater on the Broadway audience, is this school's power operative in the movies as well? I think not. Broadway audiences are notoriously pliable and faddist, while the more intransigent mass audiences respond primarily to that which moves or speaks for them. Furthermore, although on Broadway the literate play can be roughed up by the performance, in Hollywood, parts are tailored to fit personalities. What personality did the inarticulate hero assume in the movies? It is obvious that when Brando went to Hollywood he took Stanley Kowalski with him. With very little adjustment, Brando's Stanley became the paraplegic war veteran of *The Men,* the ex-prize fighter-dock worker of *On the Waterfront,* the leather-jacketed delinquent of *The Wild One,* the peasant leader of *Viva Zapata!* and even Antony in the filmed version of *Julius Caesar* (to capitalize on Brando's box office personality, Antony was changed into a sullen, beetle-browed muscle-man). Although the hero maintained, in almost every case, his identification with sexuality and violence, he could no longer be accused of cruelty or brutality.

Was it merely to the magnetism of Brando's personality that the mass audience responded, as they had responded in the past to Clark Gable, Gary Grant, and Gary Cooper? Again, I think not. Brando's personality, as he never tires of telling the press, has little in common with that of the character he plays: one of his first Broadway roles was the sensitive poet Marchbanks in *Candida* and he has lately been attempting roles of a more articulate nature. Furthermore, those actors who have imitated Brando's inarticulate style have achieved almost as much success as he.

I do not think we can escape the conclusion that Brando's spectacular film success rests to a large extent on his being one of the images (he was the original image) of the inarticulate hero. It is, in other words, to the inarticulate hero that the mass audience responds.

The most conspicuous thing about the inarticulate hero as a movie figure is that he is invariably an outcast or a rebel, isolated from friends, from parents, from teachers, from society. This is emphasized by his shabby, careless appearance; in a world of suits and ties, the leather jacket and open collar are symbols of alienation and rebellion. The main character in *On the Waterfront* is, until he is beaten up by labor hoodlums, befriended neither by police nor peers and finds consolation only in homing pigeons. Although the hero of *The Wild One* begins as the leader of a group of cyclists who terrorize a small town, he repudiates his vicious companions and is, in turn, assaulted by the furious townspeople. The young boy (James Dean) of *Rebel without a Cause* cannot gain acceptance by his adolescent contemporaries nor can he come to terms with his family until he is attacked by a juvenile gang revenging themselves for the death of their leader. The son in *East of Eden* is a pariah, doomed like Cain (with whom he is identified) to be despised by his father and rejected by the town in which he lives. The hero of *Edge of the City,* on the run from the police and alone until befriended by a paternal Negro dock worker, gets involved in a vicious hookfight with a sadistic dockyard foreman. The schoolboy in *Careless Years,* anxious to marry before he is old enough, isolates himself from everybody's love and friendship until he is soundly whipped in a fist fight with his father. The oil worker of *Giant* lives alone in a dilapidated shack, building a fortune so that he can revenge himself on the smug and settled families of the area. In *Jailhouse Rock,* the hero spends a year in jail for manslaughter where he learns to play the guitar; upon being released, he becomes rich as a rock-and-roll singer, alienating his closest friends until he is beaten up by his best friend. In each case, although the hero is a rebel against established authority, he is not necessarily identified with the lawless elements of society. He is in the middle, isolated and alone, a victim of forces he cannot understand. Frequently involved with the police, he is often in jail. Society itself is viewed as the outside of a prison, mechanical, forbidding, inhibitive, and repressive; but curiously enough the hero is trying to enter this prison, for it offers warmth and security on the inside. The obstacle is his own rebellion and before he can enter he must get involved in violence, as if in expiation for some sin. Before he can become a member of society, he must first be beaten up. In order to win—to be accepted—he first must lose.

The pattern of all these films, then, is the same: although the hero starts off on the wrong side, he is almost always converted to righteousness before the end. This is usually accomplished with the aid of his one ally in society, the girl who loves him. The girl (her face is that of Julie Harris, Natalie Wood, Eva Marie Saint, and Elizabeth Taylor, but her character doesn't vary) is frequently an adolescent and invariably virtuous and understanding. Unlike the boy, she speaks coherently (and interminably), attends school regularly, gets good grades, and is accepted from the outset by her family and friends. Most significant, she exhibits a maternal protectiveness that belies her adolescent appearance and tends to make the hero extremely dependent on her (a situation reflected in much of our popular music where the recurring motif is "I want, I need you, I love you"). The boy's actual mother has little personality, little influence on his life, and even less of a role, while the girl friend is the only one who who can control him. The disguised family romance usually found in these movies becomes, in *Giant,* more explicit. One of the main objects of dispute between Rock Hudson and James Dean is Hudson's wife, Elizabeth Taylor.

Only she offers the boy understanding and tenderness, and it is primarily for frustrated love of her that the boy fashions his revenge on the moneyed families of the town.

The antagonism which the boy feels toward society, convention, law and order is, of course, merely an extension of hostility toward his father. While Brando's films are not concerned much with family life (the isolation of the character he plays is complete), most of James Dean's films center on the family situation, a fact which accounts for a good deal of his posthumous popularity. In *East of Eden, Rebel without a Cause,* and *Giant,* Dean is found in violent combat with his father or father figure. In *Rebel without a Cause,* for example, the crucial scene occurs when the boy lashes his father for his weakness and for having no effective advice to offer him in time of trouble. In *East of Eden,* the boy is alienated by his father's indifference to him and his inability to see that his best son is not Abel, the conventional good boy, but Cain, the unconventional rebel. The boy's feelings toward his father, however, are, as we might expect, ambivalent. In one scene in *East of Eden,* the boy, whipped to indignation by his father's coldness, begins to pummel and ends by embracing him. The boy's acceptance by society at the end of these films is usually a symbol of filial reconciliation. The greatest reward the hero can achieve is acceptance by the group and the love of his father. And here we have a glimpse into the meaning of the hero's inarticulacy, for we are led to believe that his original alienation arose out of misunderstanding. Conflict is caused by a failure in communication; the boy cannot express his true feelings and therefore the father thinks him hostile. In the final scene of *East of Eden,* the father has suffered a paralytic stroke and is dying. He lies mutely on his bed (the camera shooting from above emphasizes his helplessness), his arms and lips paralyzed, able to signify assent or denial only with his eyes. Only then, when the parental authoritative voice of the father is quiet, when there can be no interruptions from him, when the fear he has instilled has been dispelled by his powerlessness, only then can the boy speak truly, coherently, and clearly, and effect understanding and reconciliation.

Ambiguous feelings toward the father (leading to hostility toward society in general) is, of course, a classic juvenile dilemma, and there can be little doubt that the inarticulate hero is fostered and cherished by the juvenile elements of our society. The striking thing to note is how effectively adolescents have been able to persuade our culture today to conform with their views of it (a recent ad for *Look* Magazine promises the life of Jesus as seen "through the troubled eyes of a teen-ager"). It is significant that not only Marlon Brando and James Dean have become spokesmen for the adolescent generation, but Elvis Presley as well; for Presley is the musical counterpart of the inarticulate hero. For the first time in recent memory, popular music has discarded intelligibility, even on the most basic level. Beginning by ignoring language, rock and roll is now dispensing with melodic content and offering only animal sounds and repetitive rhythms. In Elvis Presley, the testament of Stanley Kowalski is being realized, for, besides the physical resemblances and the explicit sexuality they share, both prophesy the ruin of culture. It is no accident that the costume of the inarticulate hero (blue jeans, T-shirts, sneakers) is primarily the same as that of the proletarian hero. The burden of protest has been handed down, as a heritage, from the one to the other. Denied the social and political outlets rebellion once was permitted to take, the adolescent is now seeing dramatized, in his music and in the movies and TV, the only rebellion left him, the Freudian protest. Although this rebellion often has an apparently happy ending with the hero securely ensconced in the bosom of his family, in reality nothing has been resolved: the hero is never seen in a mature action. The adolescent rebel never grows up; when James Dean grows to middle age, in *Giant,* he merely has some powder added to his hair.

These films, then, give the hero an appearance of growth but derive their success from catering to the anarchic impulses of the young. Inarticulacy is a symptom of this anarchy because speech is an instrument of control. To teach children to speak is to teach them to frustrate their sexual and aggressive desires. To accept this speech is to accept all the difficulties as well as all the glories that speech entails: the teachings of the father, the complexity of the world, the discipline of a developing intelligence, the gifts of tradition, history, science, and art. To reject it is to find consolation in raw feeling, in mindlessness, and in self-indulgence, to seek escape in sex and violence. In the hero's inarticulacy, we find represented the young American's fears of maturity, for to speak out—to be a speaker—is to be a man. It is to replace his father, to take the consequences of his hostility toward him, symbolically to kill him. The unnamed sin for which the hero is beaten, at the end of most of these films, is the sin against the father. When this is expiated by physical punishment, then the hero finds his way home, not to independent manhood but to the kind of security which breeds conformity and complacency.

We can see how much of the acting and the writing of the inarticulate hero is not only neurotic but conformist. The need today is not for a hero who seems to be a rebel while really conforming to an established pattern, but for a hero who, without rejecting language, tradition, education, and art—without finding consolation in the impulsive anarchy of Stanley Kowalski—can express the nonconformism which stems from a long, hard, individualistic look at the world.

Truth and Dramatic Mode
in *A Streetcar Named Desire*

Alvin B. Kernan

Both Chekhov and Pirandello created plays written in a mixture of modes which bring the individual and his suffering into relief, but they do so only by ignoring any power which transcends man and forces him to certain decisions. Some qualification of this statement is required to adjust it to Chekhov, but by and large both the dramatists discussed show humanity in a purely human setting. Man can understand himself by understanding others. Tennessee Williams recognizes this as a possibility, but he cannot, as Pirandello and Chekhov do, simply deny the validity of the realistic perspective. His plays are unresolved battles between Pirandello's stage manager and the characters, and his heroes are usually, though not always, mixtures of Dorn and Trepleff. In each of his plays, Williams poises the human need for belief in human value and dignity against a brutal, naturalistic reality; similarly, symbolism is poised against realism. But where the earlier playwrights were able to concentrate on human values, Williams has been unable to do so because of his conviction that there is a "real" world outside and inside each of us which is actively hostile to any belief in the goodness of man and the validity of moral values. His realism gives expression to this aspect of the world, and *A Streetcar Named Desire* is his clearest treatment of the human dilemma which entails the dramatic dilemma. We are presented in *Streetcar* with two polar ways of looking at experience: the realistic view of Stanley Kowalski and the "non-realistic" view of his sister-in-law, Blanche DuBois. Williams brings the two views into conflict immediately.

From *Modern Drama* 1, no. 2 (September 1958). © 1958 by the University of Toronto, Graduate Centre for the Study of Drama.

When Blanche first arrives in the "Elysian Fields" she is terrified by its shabbiness, animality, and dirt, and, pointing vaguely out the window, says, "Out there I suppose is the ghoul-haunted woodland of Weir!" Her sister, Stella, replies, "No, honey, those are the L and N tracks." This is the basic problem which has kept the modern theater boiling: Is the modern world best described as a "ghoul-haunted woodland" or a neutrally denominated something like "The L and N tracks?" The question is kept open in *Streetcar* in a number of ways. Stanley, suspicious about the amount of clothes and jewelry that Blanche has, decides that she has cheated Stella, and therefore himself, of her inheritance of the old plantation. He, however, mistakes rhinestones for diamonds, junk jewelry for genuine, imitation furs for white fox, and a mortgage-ridden, twenty-acre, decayed plantation for a cotton kingdom. The mistake is the mistake of the realist who trusts to literal appearances, to his senses alone.

In the course of the play Williams manages to identify this realism with the harsh light of the naked electric bulb which Blanche covers with a Japanese lantern. It reveals pitilessly every line in Blanche's face, every tawdry aspect of the set. And in just this way Stanley's pitiless and probing realism manages to reveal every line in Blanche's soul by cutting through all the soft illusions with which she has covered herself. But it is important to note that it is an artificial light, not a natural one, which reveals Blanche as old and cheap. She is so only when judged by a way of looking at things which insists that the senses are the only true measure of things, and only that is real which is a "thing."

But while the play makes clear the limitations of realism as an approach to experience, it makes it equally clear that this view must be accepted, however much we may dislike it; and Williams here and in his other plays dislikes it a great deal. The "realistic" point of view has the advantage of being workable. Blanche's romantic way of looking at things, sensitive as it may be, has a fatal weakness: it exists only by ignoring certain portions of reality. This is shown in a number of ways in *Streetcar,* principally in Blanche's refusal to face up to certain acts of her past and the present reality of her own sexual drives which she covers over with such words as "flirting." The movement of the play is towards a stripping away of these pretensions and culminates in the scene where Stanley rapes Blanche. As Stanley destroys each of Blanche's pretensions, pointing out that she didn't "pull any wool over this boy's eyes," Blanche tries desperately to telephone for help, but doesn't know the address. She turns to the window, still looking for help, and looks at the *facts:* "A prostitute has rolled a drunkard. He pursues her along the walk, overtakes her and there is a struggle. A policeman's whistle breaks it up. . . . Some moments later the Negro woman appears around the corner with a sequined bag which the prostitute had dropped on the walk. She is rooting excitedly through it." Here is reality, "raw and lurid," the animal struggle for existence which has replaced the bourgeois drawing room in the modern theater. Yet Blanche has always known these facts. Her husband turned out to be a pervert, then committed suicide. Belle Reve was mortgaged away to provide for the "epic fornications" of her ancestors, and death in its most terrible shapes made its home in her house for many years. When reproached by Mitch for deception she replies, simply, "I didn't lie in my heart." Just as she had turned from the death in Belle Reve to the "life" of casual amours, so she had turned away from the misery of "reality" to her romantic evasions. But Stanley hates her, has to prove his dominance, and after analyzing her in his own "realistic" terms, rapes her. Reality has forced itself on her, and she has no way left to travel except madness and death. She cannot live with what Williams and most men of our time unhappily regard as reality.

But it remains for Stella to make a choice. She stands between these two, for they are the pure products of their respective views while Stella, like most humans, participates in both, born kin to the "romantic" and married to the "realistic." Her moral sense is still active, for she points out to Eunice that "I couldn't believe [Blanche's] story and go on living with Stanley." Eunice's answer contains the dreadful truth of our times, "Don't ever believe it. Life has got to go on. No matter what happens, you've got to keep on going." Man, then, says the play, has a moral sense and an aesthetic sense which looks on the world and names it correctly "The ghoul-haunted woodland of Weir," but such knowledge is useless though not untrue. Useless because you can only live in that Woodland if you rob it of all its terrors by giving it the neutral and spiritually empty denomination of "The L and N tracks." This is the pragmatic test, and behind it lies the only "truth" that Williams will maintain, "you've got to keep on going."

For Williams, as for Pirandello, the "truth" of Nature is undefinable. He only knows that the face it turns toward us is brutal and savage, the "real camino," not the "Camino Real." But rather than trying to penetrate it he falls back on showing that "realism" is simply a man-made mode of coming to terms with a world it could not otherwise face. Yet Williams's violent fluctuations between expressionism and a Zolaesque realism, his delight in rich symbolism even in the midst of his most realistic plays, suggest a sensitive awareness of absolute moral values and of a Nature which transcends the misery of the "Elysian Fields."

A Streetcar Named Desire— Nietzsche Descending

Joseph N. Riddel

To see *A Streetcar Named Desire* as a realistic slice-of-life is to mistake its ambitious theme; to find it social protest is to misread the surface, for just as in *The Glass Menagerie,* Williams gets in his social licks while groping for a more universal statement. It is not, however, in its subthemes that *Streetcar* fails but in its overabundant intellectualism, its aspiration to say something about man and his civilization, its eclectic use and often contradictory exploitation of ideas. Williams has been called neo-Lawrencean, placing him in that assemblage of revived romantics and primitives in revolt against a sodden, effeminate age, but he is a Nietzschean as well, if in a very imperfect and perhaps overimpetuous way.

In *Streetcar,* as in several other plays, Williams borrows from Nietzsche in great chunks, often undigested, using his sources with that liberal freedom that has become characteristic of the American artist in search of a theme. Readers of *Streetcar* are soon aware of the problems this creates, for they are faced at the beginning by a welter of symbols—both linguistic and theatrical—that force upon the realistic surface a conscious, almost allegorical pattern. Williams has, at various times, had less success with the integration of his excessive symbolism and his theme, as in the satyr-like spiritualism of *The Rose Tattoo* or the panic-homosexual-psychoanalytic motif of *Suddenly Last Summer.* But even in *Streetcar* one must begin with a contradiction between his intellectual design and the militant primitivism of the theme; or to use a philosophical gloss, one must begin with Nietzsche's Apollonian-Dionysian conflict, in an almost literal sense.

From *Modern Drama* 5, no. 4 (February 1963). © 1963 by the University of Toronto, Graduate Centre for the Study of Drama.

Williams has offered what he considers a serious rationale for his kind of drama in "The Timeless World of a Play," with which he prefaced an edition of *The Rose Tattoo*. The argument is dubious but revealing. As if he had misinterpreted Eliot's remark, that art expresses a primitive truth which uses the phenomena of civilization because that is all it has to use, Williams makes a plea for the drama as a nontemporal stage whose characters are removed from and purified of their distracting social contexts. The play, he insists, arrests time, snatching the "eternal out of the desperately fleeting," penetrating beyond the social façade to the innate man beneath. Anyone familiar with the devices of *The Glass Menagerie* will recognize that he is to take a cue from the opening and closing sequences and filter out the tawdriness of the middle, the mundane stuff that blights the purity of the characters' hearts and actions. Life, it implies, is maligned by the conditions of living. There is more than social protest here, and there is certainly no area for the tragic.

This strangely persistent romantic notion that the idea of man is some prerational, mystical, universal oneness which civilization with its artificial forms travesties is indifferent to the artist's strategic assumption that between man and his conditions there is indeed a plausible and symbolic connection. What Kenneth Burke has termed the strategy of scene-act ratio is certainly fundamental to a fully realized stage, from the mythic to the realistic—as Francis Fergusson's important study, *The Idea of a Theater,* proves. (One can make this observation, I think, without being callous about social inequity or injustice, without saying that each man deserves his environment.) Williams himself depends extensively on the symbolic ratio of character to scene, yet he seems to ask for two contradictory things: that we endure his realistic surface—and indeed be entertained and informed by it—and that we respond more truly by extirpating the temporal and spiritually involving ourselves in the purified world beneath. In effect, the symbolic scene should add meaningful dimensions to the play, yet not be a temporal setting at all. Furthermore, he is insisting that in the drama individuation of character is only a convenience and that character finally resolves into the archetypes of a morality play—or better, a premorality dance of life. This is something else again than saying that a character must be universal; it claims that he is pure essence. In sum, it is a rather narrow variation on the prevailing critical thesis of drama as ritual, only Williams, instead of making the valid observation that characters constitute parts of a whole in the play, steps outside drama to postulate a spiritual, primordial idea of man which the play evokes.

In *The Birth of Tragedy*, Nietzsche describes the difference between the chorus and the virgins bearing laurel branches, in his characteristic Greek play, as a symbolic antithesis of the Dionysian and the Apollonian: the one characterized by a oneness of passion and metaphysical character, the other by restraint, order, and by individuation of character. His metaphysical tension between the Dionysian and the Apollonian natures is, in the simplest terms, his definition of tragedy; but as Walter Kaufmann has convincingly shown, to accentuate the Dionysian at the expense of its antithesis, as is popularly done, is to misread Nietzsche's famous metaphor. Indeed, says Kaufmann, Nietzsche is the Apollonian at heart, who has come to recognize the effeteness of civilization that exhausts or extirpates its vital creative energies (its Dionysian self) in empty forms, that sacrifices vitality for order. The Dionysian spirit, then, he finds necesssary but potentially chaotic, unless channelled and put to creative use by the Apollonian. In Greek drama at its height Nietzsche discovered just the proper tension—so necessary to his conception of man's tragic dignity—before the intrusion of Socratic reason, admirable as it was, led to a forced exclusion of the Dionysian vitality, and subsequently, in secular epigenism and Christianity, to an ethical world view that sought to suppress all disordered passions. The point of all this is that Nietzsche, the supposed progenitor of postethical romanticism, is an antagonist of romanticism, which he repudiated in a later preface to *The Birth of Tragedy* as a kind of unrestrained, chaotic investment in emotion for emotion's sake. In his later work, Kaufmann shows, Nietzsche reconstructed Dionysus in the character of an ideal divinity (a combination of Dionysus-Apollo), so that the repudiated Dionysus and the one with whom Nietzsche at last identified himself are two different gods. In sum, Nietzsche's conception was dialectical, Dionysus needing Apollo like the id an ego, or vitality form; and ultimately the two blend in an ideal of tragic beauty. It is the influence of a Jung, with his radically romantic world of archetypes, that has done so much to motivate our artists' return to the primitive, but the misplaced emphasis on Nietzsche's Dionysus is no less important.

Willfully or not, Williams seems to commit the error of popular misinterpretation, not in the sense that he writes a drama to the Nietzschean tune but that he exploits Nietzsche's metaphor to elucidate and justify his own vaguely formed vision of man. At times his play gains intensity of realization from his obsession with the conflict between creative impulse and civilized decorum; on other occasions it suffers from a divisiveness caused by its lack of tension, its undialectical character, its deliberately one-sided argument. This very lack of tension—thematic not dramatic—precludes tragedy and leaves us in a very startling way with a thesis play of sorts and a series of violent if symbolic actions.

The setting of *Streetcar* is a combination of raw realism and deliberate fantasy, a world very much of our society yet timeless and innocent, without ethical dimensions. Williams's evocation of a mythical Elysia suggests a world of the guiltless, of spring and sunlight (though his is shaded, a night world), a pre-Christian paradise where life and passion are one and good. The "Elysian Fields" is New Orleans in several senses: the Elysia where life is pursued on a primitive level beyond or before good and evil. This, I think, must be insisted upon, for the play is a deliberate outrage against conventional morality, a kind of immoralist's protest in the manner if not the style of Gide. The impressionistic scene, lyrical and with an aura of vitality that "attenuates the atmosphere of decay," is a Dionysian world of oneness, where there is an "easy mingling of races" and the pagan chromatics of a "blue piano" provide rhythms for a Bacchic revel.

One does not have to force his interpretation. The humorous vulgarity of the opening section is self-consciously symbolic, abrupt on the level of realism but carefully designed to signify the play's two worlds. Stanley's appearance in his masculine vigor, carrying a "red stained package from the butcher's," competes with the mythical aura of the scene. The implied virility of his gesture in tossing the package to Stella, her suggestive response, and the carefree vigor of their unconcern with time defines succinctly a kind of world that is immediate yet infused with an intensity beyond the real. The scene then pans down on Blanche in her demure and fragile dress, garishly overrefined, overwhelmed by life, out of place in Elysium. She has arrived, we learn, by way of a Freudian streetcar named "Desire," transferring to one called "Cemeteries." The psychoanalytic devices are obvious: Stanley's gesture is vital—prurient yet pure; Blanche on her figurative streetcars has been a pawn of the phallus of desire. If she is a cliché of southern literature, she is likewise the incarnate death wish of civilization. Williams takes his epigraph from Hart Crane's "The Broken Tower," and perhaps also his streetcar from Crane's "For the Marriage of Faustus and Helen," though the poet's work soon jumps its Freudian tracks to become his Faustian artist's symbolic conveyance to a Helen-ideal. Like Crane, Williams finds love in man's "broken world" a "visionary company," an "instant in the wind" suffused with time's desperation. Blanche and Stanley become antiphonal figures in a choric exchange of ideas. The Freudian-Nietzschean paraphernalia operate in close conjunction as a massive assault on the futility of our civilized illusions, which Williams always portrays as both necessary and self-destructive.

The Apollonian-Dionysian motif is vigorously accentuated, but not exactly to Nietzsche's purpose. Blanche, as her name implies, is the pallid, lifeless product of her illusions, of a way of life that has forfeited its vigor through what she later calls her family's "epic fornications," perversions of a healthy procreative sex. Her "Belle Reve," the family plantation, rests in Apollo's orchard, "Laurel," Mississippi. She is in every sense the sum of an exhausted tradition that is the essence of sophistication and culture run down into the appearance that struggles to conceal rapacity. Her life is a living division of two warring principles, desire and decorum, and she is the victim of civilization's attempt to reconcile the two in a morality. Her indulgent past is a mixture of sin and romance, reality and illusion, the excesses of the self and the restraints of society. Williams has followed Nietzsche in translating what is essentially metaphysical hypothesis into a metaphor of psychological conflict. Her schizoid personality is a drama of man's irreconcilable split between animal reality and moral appearance, or as Freud put it figuratively, a moral conflict of id against ego and super-ego. Blanche lives in a world of shades, of Chinese lanterns, of romantic melodies that conjure up dream worlds, of perversions turned into illusory romances, of alcoholic escape, of time past—the romantic continuity of generations to which she looks for identity—and of Christian morality that refines away, or judicially and morally vitiates, animal impulse. Thus, she is driven by guilt over the very indulgences that give Stanley's life a vital intensity.

As her antiself, Stanley is as consciously created. Born under the sign of Capricorn, the Goat—as Blanche was born under the sign of Virgo—he is, according to the stage directions, a veritable Pan-Dionysus, the "gaudy seed-bearer," the embodiment of "animal joy" whose life "has been pleasure with women, the giving and taking of it, not with weak indulgence, dependently, but with the power and pride of a richly feathered male bird among hens." He is identified variously with the goat, the cat, and the locomotive, three rather obvious symbols that define his sex-centered life and repeatedly disturb Blanche's tenuous psychic balance. It is revealing, too, that Blanche very early sees in Stanley a source to reinvigorate the DuBois blood. This is no genetic plan but, on Blanche's part, a pathetic hope for the revival of the old dissipated values. She finds her evil lying in the blood and her values in the illusions which can explain away moral indiscretions. Those who acclaimed Williams's earthly inferno mistook the symbolic scene for realism, failing to note the inverted image of a pagan Paradiso, where civilized values are in desuetude and the blood dictates a pulsating order of intensity and calm. The characters are to be judged, if at all, in degree to their response to the rhythm.

The love of Stanley for Stella describes precisely this rhythm of violence and reconciliation, and it exists beyond Blanche's ken. The jazz motif which alternates with the polka music—in contrast to Blanche's affinity for the romantic waltz—establishes the primitive norm to which each character adapts or suffers a dissonant psychic shock. All the old devices are here. The animal appetite is equated with the spiritual appetite for wholeness, and must be satisfied on its own terms, not those of a preestablished ethic. Stanley and Stella move freely between elemental sex and mystical experience, and Williams lends to their relationship every possible symbolic device to enforce the mystical oneness of their union. On the other hand, Blanche's neurotic reveries emerge from the internal drama of conflicting passions caused by her moral conscience. They are to be described, I suppose, in the familiar psychological terms of repression and transference, though the drama seems to lay the cause, not the cure, at the foot of consciousness and reason. Blanche's obsessive bathing is a nominal gesture of guilt and wished-for redemption, which becomes one of the play's recurrent symbols, along with the piano, locomotives, cats, telephones, and drink.

Alcohol plays a dual role. If it is one source of Blanche's hysterical escape from moral contingencies, it is likewise the stimulant of the Bacchic rites that punctuate Stanley's life. Drunkenness, indeed, is the physiological analogue for Dionysian ecstasy, as the dream-illusion symbolizes the Apollonian state. Blanche drinks to induce illusion, to extirpate moral contradictions that stand between her and the pure "Belle Reve." But for Stanley, drink induces a state of conviviality and conjugal oneness that has meaning only because it is counterbalanced by violent disturbances of irrational passion. His moments of violence are caused invariably by an external intrusion into that oneness, though violence is an integral part of the blood rhythm by which he lives. The rape scene must be read in this context, even though it is popularly recorded as a combination of unremitting realism and oversuggestive theatrics.

A closer look at a sequence of the play's middle scenes will, I think, underscore the way in which Williams exploits this primitive rhythm while moving his play along in temporal sequence. Scene 3 opens with some down-to-earth conversation at the poker table, set in the timeless impression of what the stage directions call a "Van Gogh" canvas. Blanche and Stella have gone out for dinner, a show, and drinks. They return soon after the scene opens, bringing into the masculine world a feminine interruption. Blanche's conduct is vulgarly suggestive, and a combination of her sexual gestures toward Mitch and her playing of the radio—first the derivative and conventionalized Latin rhythms of Xavier Cugat, then Viennese waltzes—leads conclusively to Stanley's violence upon Stella. The motivation here is not unsubtle. Stanley is incited to toss the radio out the window, and Stella responds with an uncharacteristic reproach: *Drunk-drunk-animal thing, you!*" Stella for the moment echoes Blanche, judging her husband by the values of her old life, censuring the animal vitality that has rescued her from Blanche's effete world. The dramatic rhythm that completes the scene was the perfect opportunity for Brando's "'method." Stanley's impulsive beating of Stella, her withdrawal, the moments of waiting while Stanley bellows goat-like in the wings, and the animal sensuality of their reconciliation fulfills the pattern of sexual will that concludes in a transcendental ecstasy of love. At the end Stella is once more within her husband's primitive embrace, to which she brings the spiritual, even cosmic, balance that his unformed vigor demands. But Blanche sees the whole affair only as "violence," upon her decorous sensibility and "Belle Reve." The real violence is the forced recognition of the conflicting drives within herself.

Scene 4 opens with the dramatic contrast between Stella and Blanche, the one "narcotized" like the face of an "Eastern idol," by her union of the previous night, the other pressed to the edge of anxiety. The entire scene is a drama of misunderstanding, accentuated by Blanche's wild but purposeless effort to rescue her sister, and thus the family, from animalistic forces. At one point she is driven to protest against Stella's mystical indifference to the night's affair by asking if her sister had cultivated a "Chinese philosophy," and one is not to miss the suggestion of identity between the Oriental calm and the sexual holiness of the two lovers. The scene moves through a series of neurotically aimless gestures on Blanche's part to a frenetic conclusion in her diatribe against an animalistic world. Immediately before the outburst, the cleavage between the two worlds is underlined:

> STELLA: But there are things that happen between a man and a
> woman in the dark—that sort of make everything else
> seem—unimportant. *(Pause)*
> BLANCHE: What you are talking about is brutal desire—just—

> Desire!—the name of that rattle-trap streetcar that bangs
> through the Quarter, up one old narrow street and down
> another . . .
> STELLA: Haven't you ever ridden on that streetcar?
> BLANCHE: It brought me here.—Where I'm not wanted and
> where I'm ashamed to be.

Love is the mystical leaven that for Stella—who, one presumes, is the ideal polarity of Stanley's realistic self—elevates the animal to the spiritual and makes them one. Uncomprehendingly, Blanche bursts out "plainly" against man's "anthropological" heritage, concluding her argument, that Stella must join the legions of culture, with a revealing plea: "Don't— don't hang back with the brutes!" There is implicit in Blanche's remarks— made against the background of the inevitable train whistle, while Stanley stands in the wings—the call of history and progress, and the Apollonian illusion of reconciliation through culture, the arts, beauty. Against this rhetoric Williams juxtaposes the action of Stanley as a reminder of the necessary vitality in any creative dream, the incipient animal within the human. The conclusion of the scene once again resolves into the passionate order of sexual transcendence, leaving Blanche pathetically and helplessly within the hollow ring of her argument.

Scene 5 offers much of the same, with Blanche's quest for escape from reality played off against the fight between Steve and Eunice, which ends in a reconciliation of "goat-like screeches" while Blanche makes seductive gestures toward a bewildered newsboy under the illusion of medieval romance. And scene 6, after an interlude of Blanche's forced prudery to stave off Mitch and her own irrepressible desires, ends in a violent confession of her horror at the suicide of her homosexual husband. Confession here acts to release her momentarily into the ecstasy of union with Mitch, which in turn leads only in the subsequent scene to guilt, ritualistic bathing, and the intense clash of Stanley's brute truths about her past and Blanche's "make-believe" rationalizations. The structure of these scenes is sound and predictable, if not sensational. There is no act division in the play, perhaps because the theme disallows a syllogistic progression of human actions in time, while demanding a recurring pattern of conflict and reconciliation that accords with the natural rhythms of passion. Realistically viewed, Stanley's world is a dreadfully boring repetition of acts, but symbolically, it fulfills a timeless, ritualistic cycle. In a sense, the progressive action required by the play's realism is at odds with the archetypal inner action, which is no better revealed than in the contradictory function of the climax.

The rape that concludes scene 10 serves a double structural purpose of resolving that scene in a moment of passion and bringing the play to its climax. There is some confusion, however, between the rape as a plausible realistic act and as a symbolic ravishing of the Apollonian by the Dionysian self. For if the play's symbolic conflict is to be resolved, as is suggested by Stanley's cryptic statement to Blanche that "We've had this date with each other from the beginning," the final scene is not so clear in its implications. Blanche, in her psychologically ingrown virginity, is driven further into herself and her dream, not released, and is handed over to Williams's modern priest, the psychoanalyst, for care. There is an unclear mingling of themes here. Blanche at first withdraws from the doctor and matron—stereotyped, masculinized symbols of the state institution—only to capitulate to the doctor when he personalizes himself by removing his professional appearance. It is, then, suggested that Blanche is to be returned to the world, the one outside Stanley's and Stella's Elysium of mystical "love," where the necessity of illusion plays its ambiguous role. Stanley's act becomes in this context an egregious breach of morality—yet the play's conclusion obscures moral judgment.

Blanche, of course, comes to symbolize a civilized world that cannot face its essential and necessary primitive self, and thus exists in a constant state of internecine anxiety. Unlike suppliants of the Dionysian cult, she cannot devour the god whose self is the wafer of regeneration. And Williams offers, as he does elsewhere, the psychoanalyst as surrogate artist-priest, who must reconstruct the fragments of personality by absolving conflict and its attendant guilt. I hesitate to conceive Williams's conclusion in strict psychological terms, for he tempers psychoanalysis with a rather indeterminate mysticism. His analyst-priest is not the Freudian doctor whose purpose is to purge the irrational and reorient the self by making suppressed conflicts conscious and intelligible. This seems to be the human gesture of the analyst in *Suddenly Last Summer,* but even there Williams conceives of him as a kind of artist, remolding one personality out of the wasteful fragments of another. Williams indicates no clear trust in the rational solution. Blanche's fate and the future of her world remain ambiguous, but Stanley and Stella are reconciled by a dual motivation: Stella by the illusion that she must unquestioningly accept things as they are and not complicate them with moral suspicions; Stanley by an animal need that provides spiritual fulfillment. If the Dionysian self never senses conflict, he remains nevertheless a marginal figure, his ecstatic world beyond our realization. We are left with Blanche's pathos, and the ambiguous suggestions that through "love" she will be returned not to the emptiness of "Belle Reve" but to a civilized world of more substantial illusions. If she is the tragic victim of a world of unrestrained animal appetite, she must regain, even through compassion and understanding, some of the vitality (and thus the primitivism) exhausted by her heirs. And Stanley's world is left, in the play's concluding words, to repeat itself timelessly in a ritual of "seven-card stud," which must stand as a reproach to if not a solution for the etiolated rituals of a civilization that excludes the realities of the blood.

The confusions of *Streetcar* must be attributed, it seems to me, to three things; the play's insistence on an amoral scene, in which the Dionysian rhythm is retailed as a norm; the use of psychological motifs to authenticate primitivism; and the deliberate exploitation of intellectual themes and symbols in the cause of anti-intellectualism. Williams's rejection of contemporary civilization takes the easy form of repudiating the moral masks which suffocate natural man, but he in no way envisions the human tensions that Nietzsche found so integral to man's tragic dignity, nor does he offer in contrast a plausible antithesis to his rejection of civilization—except a vaguely subscribed "love." This is not to say that one should expect Williams to provide either moral or intellectual answers. But to offer the purely Dionysian as a primitive order beyond morality is essentially a negative commentary, even though Williams presumes to stress an innate good in vitalism. The dialogue that constitutes tragedy is stifled, and with it Blanche's cry.

Williams fabricates his Dionysian norm without the judicious insight he employed in *The Glass Menagerie,* where the individual rises above the world's decadence by coming to moral terms with himself and the bitter realities of that world. In the purely Dionysian world, as Nietzsche pointed out and as Williams fails to grasp, individuality must be sacrificed to the universal unconscious and the tensions of dramatic conflict dissolved into chaos. Dionysianism pure is chaos and not simply the primitive order suggested in the rise and fall of blood passions. Universal innocence forfeits moral judgment, for innocence is capable of the extremes of action (including both good and evil) and thus escapes morality. Williams disallows the moralist's conclusions against Stanley's world. It is amoral (primitive and thus chaotic and partial) but made whole at least through the spiritual complement of Stella. Her role, which seems to be defined with calculated purpose early in the play, never develops functionally, and her action in the final scene fails to clarify the play. This attenuation of Stella's role is a major factor in the play's unresolved conclusion. Thus, Stanley's unpalatable world is not to be seen as rapacious but as part of the essential and inescapable reality of things. What Williams misses, in attaching now a moral judgment, now symbolic innocence to his animal functionaries is that his final scene does insinuate moral predilections while the substance of the play has obviated the moral scene for the ritualistic. Blanche's world, our world, begs for sympathy in its very throes. Williams, having attended its funeral, is loath to depart the grave, for he discovers too late that he can return only to Stanley's virile but chaotic game. The play shocks not where it is supposed to—by a deft inversion of the prevailing norms, as in Gide's *The Immoralist*—but in its realism, which it does not successfully manage to suspend. *Streetcar* is torn asunder, like Orpheus by the Maenads, by overextended symbolism and an excess of self-consciousness. The simile is not altogether unrelated to Williams's total achievement.

The Tragic Downfall
of Blanche DuBois

Leonard Berkman

Though the extent to which *A Streetcar Named Desire* exemplifies traditional tragedy may command increasing attention as this paper progresses,
a demonstration of that idea is not the central aim at hand. It is, rather,
one fragment of the question of tragic stature that most concerns us here:
the terms according to which "victory" may be considered within the heroine's grasp, the course of her struggle toward victory, and the pivotal
moment in which the struggle turns to defeat.

Especially after the late 1940s it became commonplace for critics to
talk of the ubiquitous "common man" of modern American drama, one
who is already defeated at the outset of the play's action, who struggles at
best passionately but always futilely, and who is always too low in man-
kind's moral (if not occupational) hierarchy to manage any semblance of
downfall, let alone a downfall with tragic impact. Whereas Arthur Miller
tried doggedly to develop a sense of tragedy within such dismal boundaries, insisting upon the commonness of his protagonists while insisting
too that "victory" remained nevertheless possible for them, Tennessee
Williams turned feverishly toward opposite aims. Enlisting the array of
forces—temporal and eternal, comprehensible and beyond human ken—
against which the heroic struggle must be waged, *A Streetcar Named Desire*
is an inspired refutation of the linking of modern American drama with
the common man.

Despite what humorous irony exists in any view of Blanche DuBois
as typical of the average United States citizen (particularly when that view

From *Modern Drama* 10, no. 3 (December 1967). © 1967 by A.C. Edwards.

is not reconciled with the likewise popular outcry that "life is just not as awful" as Tennessee Williams paints it) a noting of the terms according to which Blanche can be said to share in the common man's state of defeat is immediately worthwhile. A subsequent penetration into what such a view falls short of perceiving will then achieve even sharper focus.

For a thorough account of what he calls Williams's "unsparing" analysis of Blanche, turn to John Mason Brown:

> Her abiding tragedy comes neither from her family's dwindling fortunes nor from her widow's grief. It is sprung from her own nature. From her uncontrollable duplicity. From her pathetic pretensions to gentility even when she is known as a prostitute in the little town in which she was brought up. From her love of the refined when her life is devoted to coarseness. From the fastidiousness of her tastes and the wantonness of her desires. From her incapacity to live up to her dreams. Most particularly, from her selfishness and her vanity, which are insatiable.
>
> (*Dramatis Personae*)

Mr. Brown appears willing to apply "tragedy" to Blanche's situation despite his not finding her character inspiring in the least, and despite his not remarking upon even one instance of Blanche's self-awareness or effort at overcoming "her own nature." Were Blanche merely what Brown describes her to be, Williams would not have been the virtuously objective playwright Brown praises him for being in his restraint from moral pronouncement upon Blanche. Williams would, instead, have been inexcusably indulgent in not acknowledging that he had more properly in Blanche a subject for easy satire.

There are faulty defenses of Blanche that must be dismissed before a more pertinent appraisal of her can be attempted. At the core of these defenses is the deference to Blanche as representative of the artist. She is, after all, an English teacher, she values "culture," she is sensitive, she opposes Stan's brutishness. Above all, she is misunderstood. The enveloping effect of Williams's play, when it is interpreted from that perspective, is to generate intense self-pity among all those spectators who have thought of themselves as fragile, gifted, and rejected. To undermine such an interpretation, all one need do is ask how well Blanche *does* represent the artist: Wouldn't it have been more characteristic, even of the stereotype of the creative person, for Blanche to take a detached but energetic interest in observing an area of life hitherto unknown to her? Further, wouldn't Blanche need to be attacked by Stan primarily for her desires to beautify, to trans-

mit knowledge and experience, to make people more humane to one another? (On the contrary, even what might have been a sign of the artist,
the Chinese paper lantern, symbolizes in the play less beauty than conceal-
ment.) Finally, were Blanche indeed to represent the artist, where could
her struggle on behalf of art be said to reach its peak and then its defeat?
Where, in fact, could she be said, *as an artist,* to be struggling?

Not all who claim Blanche to be an artist are her partisans, yet some
of these critics make of Blanche an even greater symbol: that of Civilization writ large, its survival severely threatened by Stan, the Savage State.
In connection with so clear-cut a polarity between the two major protagonists, an ambiguity is nevertheless felt regarding the placement of Williams's sympathies: Is Williams making as much a "Lawrencian" plea for
primitive, spontaneous passion to return to dominance in his audiences'
lives as he is, simultaneously, making a plea for the safeguarding of torn,
sophisticated souls? The question's irrelevance to *Streetcar* bespeaks the ask-
ers' neglect of what concerns became crucial to Williams and to the United
States after World War II. To use only the most obvious illustration, how
could *any* contemporary, intelligent playwright be thought, in the after-
math of the war, to accept such evidence of sensitivity and of education as
an interest in poetry and an aversion to vulgarity as his basis of distinguishing the marks of civilization from the marks of savagery? Has it not
become apparent in our own time, as could never have been as apparent to
most people before, that widespread education no more diminishes man's
inhumanity to man than it diminishes man's misunderstanding of man? In
quick demonstration, Stan shows as much *understanding* of Blanche as she
of him.

Clearly, then, if an argument is to be put forth that Blanche does *not*
begin and proceed and end at the same low point, that argument must
hinge on a value that still remains to Williams and to his tragedy. Decid-
edly there is such a value, one that American dramatists of the late 1940s
and 1950s cling to desperately (Miller, the most important exception.)
This is *the belief in intimate relationships* (the establishing of the complex net-
work of human love at least on a one-to-one basis) *as paramount among life's
pursuits.* Not only is Blanche's struggle to achieve intimacy central to the
tensions of the play, but the very difficult, classically noble means which
she must exert to achieve it—the admitting of humiliating truths, the giving of compassion in the face of shock, the learning to moderate her life
so that her continued individuality is compatible with the individuality of
others—stand in testament to a by no means peculiarly midtwentieth century view of heroism. Conventionally phrased, can he who strives for or-

der in his society succeed if he cannot bring order to his own house? What *is* peculiar to the point of view of the 1940s and 1950s is the emphasis on that latter, domestic order and the idea that its pursuit is sufficient unto itself. This attitude is not the social apathy, the pessimism regarding collective human endeavor, that it might be conceived as being. It is, far more, the concern with the struggle at hand.

How, in accordance with this focus upon intimacy, do we chart the course of Blanche's life on stage? First, in attending to the state of her struggle for intimacy at the outset of *Streetcar's* action, it is necessary to note the extent of her experience with intimacy up to the time of her arrival in New Orleans. Of Blanche's relationship with her family while her parents were alive, Williams has Blanche and Stella make scarcely a comment. It is Blanche's more fervently described devotion to their family and to their family home, Blanche's frank hatred of the wastrel fornication of her male relatives, and Blanche's talkativeness leaving little opportunity for Stella's own words, which alone distinguish her own family relationship from Stella's. Implicit in Blanche's onstage relationship with her younger sister, however, is a family mutually giving of intermittent and sudden affection to one another while being mutually reluctant, apart from Blanche's quickness to express hostile emotion, to be truthful to one another. That Blanche and Stella do not view with amazement Blanche's turning for refuge to Stella's home offers some, but not enough, counterweight to the fact that Blanche and Stella have made not one attempt to see each other, and have exchanged only untruthful letters, ever since Stella left their Mississippi plantation and married Stan.

Blanche's youthful marriage to Allan Grey matches in a crucial respect the limits to intimacy that held sway in Blanche's family: Whatever the goodness of Blanche and Allan's exchanges of affection and shared poetic sensibilities, a solidification of their intimacy through the telling of certain truths never succeeded in coming about. It is not the existence of Allan's homosexuality that signals the failure of Blanche's marriage; it is, rather, that Blanche must uncover this information by accident, that Blanche is incapable of responding compassionately to this information, that in short there *never* existed a marriage between them in which Allan could come to her in full trust and explicit need. Though Blanche does turn wholly to that kind of fleeting "intimate" affair with strangers in which no deeply personal demands can be placed upon her, the point *Streetcar* makes is not that Blanche's fall has as its source the collapse of her marriage, but instead that, immersed in dishonesty even before that collapse and nearly having yielded to it utterly, Blanche is beginning (as shown in the action of the play) to force the truth to break through. Blanche's most fundamental regret, as we see her in New Orleans, is not that she happened to marry a homosexual. Far readier to face her own responsibilities than is the similarly alcoholic Brick in the similar moral crisis presented in *Cat on a Hot Tin Roof,* Blanche's concern is more directly that, when made aware of her husband's homosexuality, she brought on the boy's suicide by her unqualified expression of disgust. In Blanche's refusal to shirk a responsibility that the conventional society of her time and place would have eagerly excused, she is doing more when she talks of her past to Mitch than simply telling him her life's story. Hoping for intimacy with Mitch, she is rising to the height that intimacy demands.

From Blanche's entrance on stage to the moment of her confession of guilt to Mitch all of the difficulties of her achieving any sort of intimate relationship come into play. To an extent, Stan and Stella have what Blanche wants. Their intimacy involves a degree of humility, spirited affection, and overt need, certainly, as well as the working out of a pattern of living generally suitable to them both. However unsuitable such a pattern might be for Blanche, she is confronted constantly with evidence of the intimacy she desires and, simultaneously, with demonstrations of how exclusive even of her partial participation such intimacy is. Blanche's behavior vis-à-vis her own sister underscores *their* incompatibility for intimacy; Stella, despite her genuine feeling for Blanche, must condescend to Blanche and must flatter her or lie to her in order to be able to get along with her, just as Blanche herself feels she must "put on airs" in order to bring herself to tolerate the situation in which she now finds herself. Although Blanche's desire to be truthful and spontaneous toward Stan and Stella provokes sporadic moments of risk, as when she admits flirting with Stan and when she impulsively kisses Stella's hand, intimacy remains beyond her reach. It is with Mitch that prospects soar.

Note in the early interaction with Mitch how the foreplay, a mixture of affectation, jocularity, and sober truth, is thoroughly in keeping with the behavior we have already seen in Blanche. (She is not "suddenly" a different woman with Mitch.) By its persistence, Mitch's unconcealed vulnerability inspires Blanche to be more openly and steadily vulnerable herself. Fearful that her satisfying him would lead to his loss of regard for her, Blanche repulses Mitch's sexual advances and creates a constant impediment to their being fully easy with one another. The evidence of Mitch's own ambivalent attitude toward sex, however, supports Blanche's fear. Tellingly, Mitch's kisses are by no means fended off by Blanche when they come, in rapid succession, in response to Blanche's story of her marriage. It is specifically the intermingling of sex with compassion that Blanche longs for; sex without compassion, that she cannot accept. Crucially, Mitch's embrace is what provokes Blanche's exclamation about God. Sex (or what passed for sex in Blanche's hotel room) has not been God, or even sufficient opiate, for her; it is, in contrast, the only kind of intimacy Mitch is, temporarily at least, capable of sharing with Blanche that can restore Blanche to grace.

Blanche maintains with Mitch the height she has reached, for in her next important scene with him she tells him of the promiscuous affairs she has had (a confession which parallels the undramatized scene in which Allan's homosexuality is revealed to Blanche, with the vital distinction that Allan is not strong enough to make the disclosure of his own accord.) Stan's persecution and exposure of Blanche to Mitch do not require this second confession from Blanche; we see proof elsewhere of Blanche's ability to persist in lying no matter what others may know. Blanche has a positive impetus for revealing her past to Mitch completely, since her difficult admissions can bind the two of them all the more deeply together.

With the second confession, however, elements of tragic irony come into ascendance. There is an assertion of T. S. Eliot's to which Williams firmly and sorrowfully assents: "Human kind cannot bear very much reality." The painful implication in this statement for Williams is that reality— in this context, intimacy—is nevertheless what human kind finds most glorious and must always pursue. There is tragic irony, in short, in that Mitch's response to Blanche's initial tackling of truth encourages Blanche to make further truthful admissions that will only, in Mitch's eyes, condemn her. Mitch, after Blanche's second confession, of course, does not embrace her tenderly again; he calls her dirty and demands his sexual due.

There is irony, too, in that the first confession does not involve a guilt Mitch can fully understand; the second confession does, and yet Mitch's understanding of that guilt is, at once, the barrier to further understanding.

That is the point of Blanche's downfall: the finding herself turned by her impulses toward truth in intimacy back into the whore-image from which, through truth, she struggles to escape. Stan's capability for the rape Mitch only verbally indicates is the physical incarnation of Blanche's defeat. For again, as in her time of hotels, she *is* no longer being excluded from "intimacy" in the ordinary usage of the word; but, just as she feared, it is the act of sex itself which denies intimacy to her thereafter.

Interestingly, it is Stan now who has to take upon himself the burden of a guilty lie. Whether or not we can wholly credit Stella's declaration that she could not continue to live with Stan if she believed Blanche's accusation of rape, it is obvious that Stan is not able to admit the truth to his wife, and that his lie drives him to compound his guilt by having Blanche committed to a mental institution. Unlike Stan and Stella's earlier coming together in which sex beautifully established the forgiveness necessary for them to end their conflict, nowhere in *Streetcar* is there a more vivid illustration of the pathetic use of sex to obliterate the conscience than in the penultimate lines of the play. It is no longer from Stella that Stan can gain, and no longer from Stan that Stella can gain, the forgiveness each in their lovemaking now requires.

The irrevocable impossibility of intimacy thereafter in her life is the reality that Blanche must live with no less harshly and totally than Oedipus must live with the knowledge that he has slain his father and married his mother. A sentimentality that ignores what is basic to the turn of events in Blanche's life would have to be invoked for Blanche and for her audience to hope that there could ever still, someday, after Blanche has suffered enough perhaps, arrive a Mitch who would accept Blanche in all her guilt. Not only would Mitch's rejection of her have occurred even were he not so inordinately tied to his mother (Stan's example offers only a hint of what other varieties of rejection could occur) but, more ironically, Mitch in rejecting Blanche turns against exactly the kind of life Blanche honors him for turning against. Blanche herself would have rejected Blanche.

Blanche cannot at all be accurately seen as the weak hypocrite John Mason Brown portrays her as being; the morality she persists in avowing is not her lie. The conscious drive toward propriety and refinement that her upbringing and environment have confirmed within her are not less profoundly respected by her than the sexual and emotional longing which she had to forego propriety to satisfy. Ultimately it is neither drive that Blanche would want to yield.

In this light, is it the pathetic helplessless of insanity that Blanche demonstrates as she allows herself to be led into exile "as if she were blind" (and with no attempt at violence once the doctor has become personalized)? It is likelier that although her hopes for her own future have been crushed, and although she is moving through a siege of terror, she remains free, up through her last moment on stage, to affirm that ideal toward which she has always striven. Confronted by the presence of the doctor, she can drop the pretense that Shep Huntleigh has at last come for her; but she is affirmative in maintaining the image of herself that mocks the cardplayers for the courtesy they would never think of showing to her, and she is affirmative in fighting the medical imprisonment being forced upon her until she has gained from the doctor the perceptive gallantry and kindness she has always settled for when a mutually intimate relationship was precluded. Blanche could well have persisted in accusing Stan of raping her, and she could as well have retracted her accusation so as to try to avoid being taken away. It is a tribute to her recognition of the wider meaning of her situation that she did neither.

Blanche's approval of the doctor, her equating him with the men she has fleetingly known and to the ship doctor of her death fantasy, her asking of him no more than the "kindness of strangers," is her way of proclaiming what she now knows: Doomed by the life she has led, her struggle for intimacy has come to its end. The future she sees has only strangers, at best kind strangers, in it. Blanche's tragic power lies in her ultimate acceptance of that very future she has fought so painfully, and almost successfully with Mitch, to resist. Blanche attains this acceptance with tragic dignity, forsaking her anguish but not forsaking, as the reverberations of her final statement tell us, her vision of the intimacy, her God, in whose arms she could not remain.

Tennessee Williams: Streetcar to Glory

C. W. E. Bigsby

The theatre has long been the poor relation of the American arts and Eugene O'Neill's Nobel Prize (like Sinclair Lewis's and Pearl Buck's) was a gesture having more political than cultural significance. For all the interest of Kingsley, Odets and Hellman, indeed, American drama is largely a postwar phenomenon and its new and enhanced prestige owes a great deal to a man who started his working life in a warehouse, writing poems on shoe boxes.

Thomas Lanier Williams was born on March 26, 1914. His parents were a travelling salesman and the daughter of the local minister—which may account for the strange mixture of prurience and puritanism in his work. His first play was written in 1935 and he scored a moderate local success in St. Louis with a series of plays written for a little theatre group called The Mummers.

The forties, however, opened somewhat inauspiciously. His first play intended for Broadway production, *Battle of Angels,* was withdrawn after its Boston tryout. Nevertheless in the course of the following two decades he emerged as a major dramatist and attained the two-fold distinction of being awarded a Pulitzer Prize and being banned from the public stage in Britain, surviving both experiences reasonably intact. Always controversial, his plays were welcomed not only for their unique vision but also for the frankness and vitality which they brought to a theatre all too often starved of those qualities.

Critics have often been at pains to draw a distinction between Tennes-

From *The Forties: Fiction, Prose, Drama,* edited by Warren French. © 1969 by Warren French. Everett/Edwards, 1969.

see Williams and Arthur Miller on the basis that the former is concerned with personal fears and frustrations while the latter is concerned with social issues. Yet Williams, too, has his roots in the social theatre of the 1930s while, like Miller's *All My Sons* and *Death of a Salesman,* most of his work is concerned with the plight of the individual in the modern world. The Mummers itself was a radical group and the plays which he produced for it were largely protest dramas.

The atmosphere of hysteria and violence in his work is, therefore, not merely an expression of personal neurosis. It is also a legacy which he has inherited from a theatre in which emotionalism, sentimentality, and violent action were seen as legitimate substitutes for dramatic tension. Like Miller, too, he has inherited not merely the oversimplifications of agitprop drama but also a suspicion of wealth itself. In common with Brick, in *Cat on a Hot Tin Roof,* he is in fact something of an "ass aching Puritan." Thus the division between rich and poor in his work is, for the most part, also a division between brutality and compassion, sterility and vitality. He is enough of an old-fashioned moralist, indeed, to see bodily disease as the fruit of sin. Thus the rich are frequently pictured as being eaten away from within: Boss Finley *(Sweet Bird of Youth)* apparently by tuberculosis, his daughter by syphilis, Mrs. Venable *(Suddenly Last Summer)* by madness, Jabe Torrence *(Orpheus Descending)* and even the rich but attractive Big Daddy *(Cat on a Hot Tin Roof)* by cancer. Perhaps this is why Williams, a man who sold the film rights of one of his plays for half a million dollars, is so concerned about his own health.

On the other side of the coin are the pure in heart; the poets, romantics, bohemians, and, of course, playwrights. For he has hardly written a single play which is not obliquely concerned with his own plight as a writer in a world which values only material things. When Cervantes was asked whom he intended to represent through the figure of Don Quixote he is said to have replied, "Myself." Williams might well give the same reply with regard to any of a dozen characters. So it is that in the persons of Laura Wingfield, Blanche DuBois, Alma Winemiller, we have a series of portraits of those characters for whom Williams has the greatest sympathy; those who, like himself, have been unable fully to adjust to a world in which honor, sexual passion, integrity, and compassion no longer have a place.

Williams's first Broadway success came with *The Glass Menagerie* in 1945. This play, which won the New York Drama Critics' Award, exhibits a delicacy and control frequently lacking from his later work. Perhaps this derives, in part at least, from its biographical nature, for it is an enactment of his own relationship with his mother and sister—the latter having been committed to an asylum in 1937. In the play she appears as Laura Wingfield, a crippled girl who has apparently withdrawn from a world which seems to offer her nothing but pain and humiliation. Alienated from society in general she creates her own world with her collection of glass animals.

Her mother, Amanda, is equally ill-at-ease in the real world and compensates for her drab surroundings by recalling memories of her youth in the old South. She is sufficiently alive to the economic realities of life, however, to wish that Laura would get married and to this end she encourages her son, Tom, to bring home one of his workmates. When he does so Laura is for a brief while drawn out of her private world only to be brutally thrust back into it again when the boy, a young man concerned only with the glittering world of the American Dream, confesses that he is already engaged. The play ends as Tom, a poet with a job in a shoe warehouse, finally leaves and Amanda tries to comfort her daughter.

Obviously the play has a special meaning for the playwright who had himself lived the nightmare which he describes but it also functions as an image of the world as Williams sees it. For he has said that "for me the dominating premise has always been the need for understanding and tenderness and fortitude among individuals trapped by circumstances." Clearly the play's setting—"the Wingfield apartment is . . . one of those vast hive-like conglomerations of cellular living units"—is, therefore, concerned with emphasizing not merely the physical oppressiveness of life lived in a materialistic society but also the destruction of the human spirit which seems, to Williams, a natural corollary of modern living.

Moreover, Laura herself is not merely a disturbingly accurate picture of his own sister. She stands also as an image of Williams's central theme; the destructive impact of society on the sensitive individual. Like the glass unicorn which is smashed by her unthinking "gentleman caller," she, and the delicate humanity which she represents, is, in Williams's words, virtually "extinct" in a modern world founded not on tenderness and understanding but on the dynamic cycle, "*knowledge*—zzzzpppp! Money—Zzzzppp! POWER! Wham!" Looking for compassion she is brought face to face with the brutality of a world in which there is an apparently unbridgeable gulf between aspiration and fulfillment. This is a lesson, too, which has to be learnt both by Blanche DuBois, in Williams's second Broadway success of the 1940s, *A Streetcar Named Desire,* and by Alma Winemiller, in *Summer and Smoke,* written before *Streetcar* but not performed until the following year.

Williams's world, for the most part, has the simplicity and directness of moral allegory. Good is opposed to evil, spirituality to sensuality, and the romantic to the brutally realistic. Indeed his characters are all too often simply manipulated in order to fulfill their functional roles in his modern parables. Alma Winemiller and John Buchanan, in *Summer and Smoke,* are supreme examples of this moral puppetry. Alma, we are pointedly reminded, is Spanish for "soul" and lest we miss the symbolic significance of this she is also made the daughter of the local minister. John Buchanan, on the other hand, stands for the body and predictably, therefore, must become a doctor, complete with an anatomical chart with which to preach his Lawrentian sermon on the dominance of the physical over the spiritual. This simplistic approach to symbolism even extends to the play's setting which, in dividing the stage between the doctor's house and the rectory (body and soul), projects the Manichean naiveté of the plot onto a visual plane. This misuse of symbolism has over the years become one of Williams's less fortunate trademarks, at its worst in *Camino Real* and *Night of the Iguana.* Yet in his best work Williams avoids this tendency to "write too much on the nose." Indeed in an interview which he gave in 1961 he confessed that if you "write a character that isn't ambiguous you are writing a false character, not a true one." With this remark he was in fact indicting creations of his own such as Alma, Boss Finley, and Mrs. Venable. Yet with his next play, *Streetcar,* which won both the New York Drama Critics' Award and the Pulitzer Prize, he showed that he was fully alive to the complexity of human nature and to the danger of facile moralising.

The mood of *A Streetcar Named Desire* is effectively summed up by the opening paragraph of a book which Williams greatly admired, *Lady Chatterley's Lover.* Here Lawrence had expressed his view of man's situation in the modern world: "Ours is essentially a tragic age, so we refuse to take it tragically. The cataclysm has happened, we are among the ruins, we start to build up new little habitats, to have new little hopes. It is rather hard work: there is now no smooth road into the future: but we go round or scramble over the obstacles. We've got to live, no matter how many skies have fallen." Williams's play is concerned with just such an attempt to discover a means and a purpose for life in surroundings which seem to offer little grounds for hope. As one of the characters says, "Life has got to go on. No matter what happens, you've got to keep on going."

Lawrence's influence on Williams has been plotted before but is especially important with regard to the work which he produced during the 1940s and to *Streetcar* in particular. In 1939 he had gone to Taos, New Mexico, to interview Frieda Lawrence. He had long been planning a play about Lawrence's death and this now finally took some kind of shape. Significantly he described the theme of this play, *I Rise in Flame, Cried the Phoenix,* as "a man's . . . pilgrimage through times inimical to human beings." As such it clearly anticipates not only *Streetcar* but also much of Williams's later work. In 1945 he once again turned to Lawrence, this time adapting one of his short stories but it was not until *Streetcar* that he managed fully to digest his Lawrentian lessons and incorporate them into his own perception of an America caught in transition from genteel sterility to brutal indifference.

Blanche DuBois is a thirty-year-old woman who, when young, had made a disastrous marriage. Her husband had turned out to be a homosexual and in forcing him to face this fact she had provoked his suicide. Unable to admit to what she had done or to accept the loneliness which stretches out ahead of her, she turns, like Alma in *Summer and Smoke,* to a series of casual intimacies with strangers and is finally run out of town when she seduces a sixteen-year-old boy.

At the beginning of the play she arrives in New Orleans to stay with her sister, Stella, fully aware that she no longer has anywhere else to run. The two sisters had been brought up on a southern plantation but Stella has abandoned the aristocratic pretensions to which Blanche clings so desperately. She has married Stanley Kowalski, a Polish immigrant worker, and, much to Blanche's disgust, appears to revel both in her husband's brutality and his sensuality.

Hope suddenly appears for Blanche, however, in the person of Mitch, a lumbering mother's boy. He is attracted to her and she realizes that marriage will provide a kind of answer to her problems. But she reckons without Stanley. There is an instinctual animosity between these two. Blanche responds to him with a pathetic mixture of aristocratic contempt and unsubtle flirtation, while Stanley sees in her only a threat to his own way of life. When he discovers the truth about her past, therefore, he warns Mitch off and completes her destruction by raping her as his own wife is in a hospital having his baby. The play ends as Blanche, now mentally unhinged, is led away from the apartment by a doctor and nurse, her contact with reality finally severed.

We are offered, it seems, a hopeless choice between decadence and brutality and, like Williams himself, have to pick our way through the personal treacheries and frustrations in an attempt to find something worthwhile endorsing. For if Williams rebels against the cruelty of the modern age he clearly recognizes too the irrelevance of Blanche's posturing. Yet for all that, she—and the southern tradition which she represents—obviously holds an attraction for Williams which goes beyond a romantic regret for past glory. He values the southern past, in fact, not because he has any illusions as to the nature of its justice or the quality of its life but simply because, to his mind, it represents order. Here the anarchic power of sexuality was masked behind a cultivated manner and the naked pursuit of wealth cloaked by the whole cavalier tradition of the South. Like Joseph Conrad he felt that we are saved from chaos only by the "sovereign power enthroned in a fixed standard of conduct." The ordered nature of society in turn suggested a cosmic order and purpose. Now, in the modern age, the veneer has been stripped away and the structure of society has disintegrated. The individual is forced to admit to the reality of flux, what one of Williams's characters describes as "the terrible—fast—dark—rush of events." It is this new, impersonal, world "sick with neon," which terrifies Williams and his protagonists. For, with order destroyed, the individual falls victim to what he sees as the blind illogic of much of human activity.

Williams's personal reaction is the predictable response of the artist. By the act of writing he tries to reimpose a sense of order. The creative act itself thus becomes an act of defiance, or, in another light, a form of escapism. This, indeed, is how one of his characters, significantly called simply, The Writer, justifies himself in a one-act play called *The Lady of Larkspur Lotion*—a play which in many ways anticipates *Streetcar:* "Suppose that I, to make this nightmare bearable for as long as I must continue to be the helpless protagonist of it—suppose that I ornament, illuminate—glorify it! With dreams and fancies! . . . suppose that I live in this world of pitiful fiction! What satisfaction can it give [anyone] to tear it to pieces, to crush it—call it a *lie?.* . . . There are no lies but the lies that are stuffed in the mouth by the hard knuckled hand of need, the cold fist of necessity." The same is true of his other protagonists. Some, like Tom Wingfield, Sebastian Venable, and Chris Flanders, are writers themselves; others, like Laura Wingfield, Alma Winemiller, and Blanche DuBois, are simply content to retreat into a world of illusion. Blanche, for example, invents a lover who will come and rescue her and by an act of will transforms her harsh surroundings, placing a paper lantern over the electric light and filling the place with pastel shades. But the final futility of this response is amply demonstrated in *Streetcar* when Blanche's desperate pretence is shattered by a man "as coarse and direct and powerful as the primary colors." For illusion is only effective so long as others are prepared to tolerate it. Hence there is a sad truth to the popular song which Blanche sings as a counterpoint to Stanley's revelations of her debauchery: "It's a

Barnum and Bailey world. Just as phony as it can be. But it wouldn't be make believe if you believed in me."

The real hero of the play, therefore, is Stella, for she alone is prepared to offer the necessary comfort and understanding. Like Connie Chatterley she discovers a genuine fulfillment based on sexuality but, more significantly, she thereby stumbles on the urgent need for that tenderness and compassion which, to both Williams and Lawrence, is the key to the human predicament. If she emerges also as the weakest character in the play this is because, however much he feels committed to seeking out some positive response to the modern world, Williams's sympathies are always with the weak and defeated while his admiration is always with those who manage to survive in and even dominate contemporary society. These latter—men like John Buchanan and Stanley Kowalski—are described by Williams as Promethean figures "brilliantly alive in a stagnant society." Yet for all their vitality these "Prometheans" are too much a product of the modern world to offer any real hope. John Buchanan, before his somewhat incredible *volte face*, lacks true compassion and sympathy while Stanley Kowalski's brutality towards Blanche finally disqualifies his mindless sensuality as a viable alternative. Nevertheless, despite this inhumanity, there are moments of tenderness between Stella and Stanley which clearly offer some slight hope for the future. For Williams, in surveying the postwar world, has said that "the only satisfactory thing we are left with in this life is the relations—if they're sincere—between people," love being "the closest we've come" to such a satisfying relationship. Where the modern European theatre stresses the impossibility of communication he continues to insist that some kind of contact is possible. But like Arthur Miller, in *After the Fall,* he is prepared to confess that this contact is imperfect and the love which it engenders an incomplete answer to the human condition. This, indeed, is the sense of the Hart Crane poem which Williams uses as an epigraph to *Streetcar.* For this is a poem which describes not only the desperate situation of Blanche DuBois and her fellow romantics but also the plight of a dramatist who from *Battle of Angels* onwards committed himself to a cause which perhaps seemed lost from the very beginning:

> And so it was that I entered the broken world
> To trace the visionary company of love, its voice
> An instant in the wind (I know not whither hurled)
> But not for long to hold each desperate choice.

Realism and Theatricalism in *A Streetcar Named Desire*

Mary Ann Corrigan

On the morning after the premiere of *A Streetcar Named Desire* in 1947, Joseph Wood Krutch commented: "This may be the great American play." From the perspective of more than a quarter of a century later, *A Streetcar Named Desire* appears to be *one* of the great American plays. Its greatness lies in Tennessee Williams's matching of form to content. In order to gain sympathy for a character who is in the process of an emotional breakdown, Williams depicts the character from without and within; both the objectivity and the subjectivity of Blanche are present to the audience. In *A Streetcar Named Desire,* Williams synthesizes depth characterization, typical of drama that strives to be an illusion of reality, with symbolic theatrics, which imply an acceptance of the stage as artifice. In short, realism and theatricalism, often viewed as stage rivals, complement each other in this play. Throughout the 1940s Williams attempted to combine elements of theatricalist staging with verisimilitudinous plots and characters. His experiments either failed utterly, as in *Battle of Angels* in which neither literal nor symbolic action is convincing, or succeeded with modifications, for instance by the removal of the screen device in *The Glass Menagerie*. In *A Streetcar Named Desire* Williams is in control of his symbolic devices. They enable the audience not only to understand the emotional penumbra surrounding the events and characters, but also to view the world from the limited and distorted perspective of Blanche. The play's meaning is apparent only after Williams exposes through stage resources what transpires in the mind of Blanche.

From *Modern Drama* 19, no. 4 (December 1976). © 1976 by the University of Toronto, Graduate Centre for the Study of Drama.

When the audience meets Blanche, she is at the same stage as Laura of *The Glass Menagerie:* one more of life's frustrating disappointments is enough to insure final retreat from the world. Blanche does not retreat without a struggle; the progress of her struggle determines the forward movement of the play's action. To communicate Blanche's subjective state at each stage of the action, Williams asks in his stage directions for aural and visual effects, some of which distort the surface verisimilitude of the play. Elia Kazan was careful to preserve these elements of stylization when he directed the original Broadway production. He explains: "One reason a 'style,' a stylized production is necessary is that a subjective factor—Blanche's memories, inner life, emotions, are a real factor. We cannot really understand her behavior unless we see the effect of her past on her present behavior." The setting, lighting, props, costumes, sound effects, and music, along with the play's dominant symbols, the bath and the light bulb, provide direct access to the private lives of the characters.

Williams's setting is emotionally charged and, as usual, described in great detail in the stage directions. Both the inside and the outside of the Kowalski house appear on stage. The house is in a slum in the old section of New Orleans. The backdrop designed by Jo Mielziner for the original production featured angled telephone poles, lurid neon lights, and ornately decorated facades on crumbling structures. Despite its dilapidation, Williams insists that the section *"has a raffish charm,"* especially in the blue light of the sky *"which invests the scene with a kind of lyricism and gracefully attenuates the atmosphere of decay."* Stanley is at home in this neighborhood and Stella has learned to like it, but its charm eludes Blanche, who says of it: "Only Poe! Only Mr. Edgar Allan Poe!—could do it justice!" Blanche finds the Kowalski environment cramped, foul and ugly, so unlike her childhood home, Belle Reve, "a great big place with white columns." In coming to New Orleans, Blanche is brought face to face with an ugly reality which contrasts with her "beautiful dream." To show the relation between the decadent New Orleans street life and the events inside the Kowalski flat, Williams asks that the back wall of the apartment be made of gauze to permit, under proper lighting, a view of the city alley. This wall becomes transparent in the rape scene.

Williams uses costuming, props, and lighting to convey the emotional strength of his characters and to reinforce the dichotomy between Blanche and Stanley. The overwrought, emotionally drained Blanche always wears pastels in half-lights; Stanley, the "richly feathered male bird," appears in vivid primary colors under strong, garish light. Blanche's clothes establish her uniqueness even in her first appearance on stage. Williams writes in the stage directions:

> *Her appearance is incongruous in this setting. She is daintily dressed in a white suit with a fluffy bodice, necklace, and earrings of pearl, white gloves and hat, looking as if she were arriving at a summer tea or cocktail party in the garden district. . . . There is something about her uncertain manner, as well as her clothes, that suggests a moth.*
>
> (scene 1)

Gerald Weales points out that Blanche's clothes are a characterizing device and a way of separating her from her surroundings: "Blanche is going to be destroyed by the end of the play and Williams wants her first appearance . . . to imply that end. Costume here becomes a way of foreshadowing the events to come." *(A Play and Its Parts.)* By the time Blanche appears the audience has already met the bellowing Stanley, dressed in work clothes, who hurled a bloodstained package of raw meat at his wife. Stella, despite her surprise, deftly caught the bundle; she has learned to function in this society.

The Poker Night scene also exploits the capacity of light and color to create mood. As he so often does, Williams cites an example from the visual arts as a model for the effect he wishes to create:

> *There is a picture of Van Gogh's of a billiard-parlor at night. The kitchen now suggests that sort of lurid nocturnal brilliance, the raw colors of childhood's spectrum. Over the yellow linoleum of the kitchen table hangs an electric bulb with a vivid green glass shade. The poker players—Stanley, Steve, Mitch and Pablo—wear colored shirts, solid blues, a purple, a red-and-white check, a light green, and they are men at the peak of their physical manhood, as coarse and direct and powerful as the primary colors. There are vivid slices of watermelon on the table; whiskey bottles and glasses.*
>
> (scene 3)

Williams's description seems to emphasize the vibrancy of this scene, but van Gogh's *Night Cafe*, obviously his model, is harrowing in its luridness, its color contrasts and tilted perspective suggesting moral degeneracy. Surely Williams intends the poker players to be frightening in their physical strength. Primitive tastes and pleasures are the norm in the Kowalski set, and those who fail to conform to this norm have no chance of survival.

Music and other sounds also communicate a sense of the ineluctable primitive forces that operate in the Vieux Carré. From the Four Deuces, a nearby night spot, come the sounds that express New Orleans life: blues, jazz, honky-tonk. Elia Kazan comments on the function of the "blue piano" music which is in the background of much of the action:

> The Blues is an expression of the loneliness and rejection, the exclusion and isolation of the Negro and their longing for love and connection. Blanche, too, is looking for a home, abandoned and friendless. . . . Thus the Blue piano catches the soul of Blanche, the miserable unusual human side of the girl which is beneath her frenetic duplicity, her trickery, lies, etc.

The Blues plays as Blanche arrives in the Vieux Carré and is particularly dominant when she recounts the deaths at Belle Reve (scene 1) and when she kisses the newsboy (scene 5). As Blanche is being led away to the asylum and Stella cries uncontrollably, the music of the blue piano swells (scene 11). At one point this music catches the soul of Stanley too: when Stella leaves him, and he sobs, "I want my baby," the *"'blue piano' plays for a brief interval"* (scene 3). But normally, the uncomplicated obtrusive rhythms of the honky-tonk express Stanley's personality. This music dominates the rape scene.

There is subjective as well as objective music in the play. Only Blanche and the audience hear the Varsouviana polka, which was played as Blanche's husband shot himself. The music, through its association in her memory with impending death, becomes a symbol of imminent disaster. Blanche hears it, for instance, when Stanley hands her a Greyhound bus ticket for a trip back to Laurel (scene 8). The music of the Varsouviana weaves in and out of the scene in which Mitch confronts Blanche with his knowledge of her background. Williams writes in the stage directions: *"The rapid, feverish polka tune, the 'Varsouviana,' is heard. The music is in her mind; she is drinking to escape it and the sense of disaster closing in on her, and she seems to whisper the words of the song"* (scene 9). In the same scene the polka tunes fades in as the Mexican street vendor, harbinger of death, arrives, chanting "Flores para los muertos." Reality in all its harshness and ugliness is epitomized for Blanche in these aural and visual reminders of death. She hears this music too in the last scene, when Stanley and the asylum matron corner her. Williams uses the symbolism attaching to Blanche's frequent bathing in order to further lay bare her inner nature. As an aspect of the visiting in-law joke, Blanche's "hogging" of the bathroom is amusing, and the earthy Stanley's references to his bursting kidneys add to the humor. But the serious symbolism is nevertheless obvious: "Blanche's obsessive bathing is a nominal gesture of guilt and wished-for redemption." Like her drinking, her bathing is an escape mechanism. The ritual cleansing which takes place in the tub restores Blanche to a state of former innocence. Once again she is young and pure in a beautiful world.

The bath is a particularly functional symbol in scene 7, in which it is used to reveal the dual world of Blanche's existence and the tension between Blanche and Stanley. Stella is setting the table for Blanche's birthday party, to which Mitch, the one person who offers Blanche a genuine possibility for redemption, has been invited. As the scene progresses, it becomes apparent that this birthday will be anything but happy. The festive occasion that falls flat is a staple of drama. Shakespeare, Chekhov, Pinter, and Williams use it to intensify the ironic discrepancy between appearance and reality. As Blanche bathes in preparation for the party, Stanely reveals to Stella the particulars of her sister's sordid life. The stage directions read: "*Blanche is singing in the bathroom a saccharine popular ballad which is used contrapuntally with Stanley's speech.*" The louder Stanley gets in his insistence upon the undeniable facts about Blanche, the louder Blanche sings in the bathroom. Her song asserts the capacity of the imagination to transform mere facts:

> Say, it's only a paper moon. Sailing over a cardboard sea—
> But it wouldn't be make-believe If you believed in me!
>
> . . . .
>
> It's a Barnum and Bailey world. Just as phony as it can be—
> But it wouldn't be make-believe If you believed in me!

When Stanley's recital reaches its climax with the most damning charge of Blanche's seduction of a student, "*in the bathroom the water goes on loud; little breathless cries and peals of laughter are heard as if a child were frolicking in the tub.*" Thus, the two Blanches are counterpoised. In emerging from the bathroom, Blanche immediately senses the threat that Stanley's world of facts poses to her world of illusions. Her usual contented sigh after the bath gives way to uneasiness: "A hot bath and a long, cold drink always give me a brand new outlook on life! . . . Something has happened!— What is it?" Background music reflects her fear: "*The distant piano goes into a hectic breakdown.*"

Blanche is as obsessed with lights as she is with baths. Her first request when she comes to the Kowalski home is that the overhead light be turned off; subsequently she buys a paper lantern to cover it. On one level, of course, Blanche's dislike of bright lights is a matter of vanity: dimness hides the signs of aging. But it is clear that the light bulb has a further significance, perhaps unconscious, for Blanche, who says to Mitch: "I can't stand a naked light bulb, any more than I can a rude remark or a vulgar action" (scene 3). Just as the naked light must be toned down by an artifical lantern, so every sordid reality must be cloaked in illusion. Stanley, on the other hand, likes as much light as possible; the clear cold light of day and the naked bulb reveal to him what is *real* and, therefore, what is *true*. And the *facts* of Blanche's former life, which Stanley assiduously "brings to light" for all to see are necessarily abhorrent to Blanche, who has different standards of truth. Mitch, having been "enlightened" by Stanley, tears the paper lantern from the bulb and demands to take a good look at Blanche.

> BLANCHE: Of course, you don't really mean to be insulting!
> MITCH: No, just realistic.
> BLANCHE: I don't want realism. I want magic! Yes, yes, magic!
> I try to give that to people. I misrepresent things to them.
> I don't tell the truth, I tell what *ought* to be truth. And if
> that is sinful, then let me be damned for it!—*Don't turn
> the light on!*
>
> (scene 9)

Being forced to face the kind of reality that she refuses to recognize as significant is the cause of Blanche's breakdown. In the last scene, as Blanche is led away, Stanley tears the paper lantern off the light bulb—he has no use for it—and extends it to her: "*She cries out as if the lantern was herself.*" Blanche is as delicate and pathetic as a paper lantern; she cannot deflect the hard light of Stanley's vision of reality.

The scene in which Stanley imposes his vision of reality on Blanche, the rape scene, is comprehended and accepted by the audience largely because of the visual and aural details through which psychological intangibles are made objective. At the beginning of scene 10 the audience is aware of Blanche's tenuous emotional state. Her appearance indicates that she is beginning to retreat into her world of illusions:

> *She has decked herself out in a somewhat soiled and crumpled white
> satin evening gown and a pair of scuffed silver slippers with brilliants
> set in their heels.*
>
> *Now she is placing the rhinestone tiara on her head before the mirror
> of the dressing-table and murmuring excitedly as if to a group of special
> admirers.*

Blanche, although revelling in her fantasies, is still capable of distinguishing them from actual events. In the middle of her feigned discussion with her admirers she catches sight of her face in a hand mirror, recognizes it as real, and breaks the mirror. At this point Stanley appears in his "*vivid green silk bowling shirt,*" to the tune of honky-tonk music, which continues to be heard throughout the scene. When Stanley confronts Blanche with his knowledge of her background, the abominable reality that Blanche detests begins to impinge upon her: "*Lurid reflections appear on the walls around Blanche. The shadows are of a grotesque and menacing form. She catches her breath, crosses to the phone and jiggles the hook.*" For Blanche the telephone is an avenue to a better world. When she sought what she called a "way out" for herself and Stella in scene 3, the telephone and telegraph were the means to effect her plan. Again she attempts to escape into a different world by calling her Texas millionaire. But when she can't give a number or an address, the operator cuts her off. Reality again! The stage directions indicate the result on Blanche of this thwarting of her plans: "*She sets the phone down and crosses warily into the kitchen. The night is filled with inhuman voices like cries in a jungle.*" Blanche has been sensitive to sound throughout the play. In the first act she jumped at the screech of a cat; later, when Stanley slammed a drawer closed, she winced in pain. Now "the cacophony that we hear is inside Blanche's head—imaginary sounds and real sounds turned grotesque and horrible by her fear." To make Blanche's mounting fears tangible Williams uses the scrim:

> *Through the back wall of the rooms, which have become transparent, can be seen the sidewalk. A prostitute has rolled a drunkard. He pursues her along the walk, overtakes her and there is a struggle. A policeman's whistle breaks it up. The figures disappear. Some moments later the Negro woman appears around the corner with a sequined bag which the prostitute had dropped on the walk. She is rooting excitedly through it.*

The New Orleans street figures are analogues of all that reality means to Blanche: violence, theft, immorality, bestiality. No wonder she tries to escape it. She returns to the telephone: "Western Union? Yes! I—want to— Take down this message! 'In desperate, desperate circumstances! Help me! Caught in a trap. Caught in—' Oh!" There is no escaping reality now, for its arch crusader, Stanley, is back:

> *The bathroom door is thrown open and Stanley comes out in the brilliant silk pajamas. He grins at her as he knots the tassled sash about his waist. . . .*

The barely audible 'blue piano' begins to drum up louder. The sound of it turns into the roar of an approaching locomotive.

Blanche reads the meaning of the sounds perfectly: she will be forced to become part of this world of hot music and lust. Her tormentor teases her with the spectre of her fears:

> You think I'll interfere with you? Ha-ha!
> *(The 'blue piano' goes softly. She turns confusedly and makes a faint gesture. The inhuman jungle voices rise up. He takes a step toward her, biting his tongue which protrudes between his lips.)*

Blanche's gesture of threatening Stanley with a broken bottle is the last and the easiest of the challenges she poses for him. Springing like an animal at prey, he catches her wrist: "*The bottle top falls. She sinks to her knees. He picks up her inert figure and carries her to the bed. The hot trumpet and drums from the Four Deuces sound loudly.*" Blanche's involuntary journey to the depths of sordidness results in her losing contact completely with any kind of reality. The theatrical devices, aural and visual, which represent not objective occurrence, but inner action, enable the audience to understand Blanche's ordeal and her retreat into insanity.

Williams depicts the total defeat of a woman whose existence depends on her maintaining illusions about herself and the world. Blanche is both a representative and a victim of a tradition that taught her that attractiveness, virtue, and gentility led automatically to happiness. But reality proved intractable to the myth. Blanche's lot was Belle Reve, with its debts and deaths, and a homosexual husband who killed himself because, for once, her sensitivity failed her. Blanche's "amatory adventures . . . are the unwholesome means she uses to maintain her connection with life, to fight the sense of death which her whole background has created in her." (Harold Clurman, *The Divine Pastime.*) Since "the tradition" allows no place for the physical and sensual, she rejects this aspect of her personality, calling it "brutal desire." Kazan writes: "She thinks she sins when she gives into it . . . yet she does give into it, out of loneliness . . . but by calling it 'brutal desire,' she is able to separate it from her 'real self,' her 'cultured,' refined self."

If Blanche is the last remnant of a moribund culture, Stanley is in the vanguard of a vital and different society. Even Blanche recognizes his strength when she says, "He's just not the type that goes for jasmine perfume, but maybe he's what we need to mix with our blood now that we've lost Belle Reve" (scene 2). If Blanche's philosophy cannot make room for "brutal desire," Stanley's comprehends little else. Williams describes him:

> Since earliest manhood the center of his life has been pleasure with
> women, . . . He sizes women up at a glance, with sexual classifica-
> tions, crude images flashing into his mind and determining the way he
> smiles at them.

(scene 1)

It is only fitting that Stanley destroy Blanche with sex. As Benjamin Nelson writes, sex "has been her Achilles heel. It has always been his sword and shield."

The conflict between Blanche and Stanley is an externalization of the conflict that goes on within Blanche between illusion and reality. The illusion sustaining her is her image of herself as a southern belle, a fine, cultured, young lady. The reality is a lonely woman, desperately seeking human contact, indulging "brutal desire" as an affirmation of life. Blanche's "schizoid personality is a drama of man's irreconcilable split between animal reality and moral appearance." This drama is played out not only in Blanche's mind, but between Stanley and Blanche as well. Stanley strips away Blanche's illusions and forces her to face animal reality. In doing so, he demonstrates that reality is as brutal as she feared. She has no choice but to retreat totally into illusion. Thus, the external events of the play, while actually occurring, serve as a metaphor for Blanche's internal conflict.

In pitting Blanche and Stanley against one another, Williams returns to his oft-told tale of the defeat of the weak by the strong. But, for a change, both figures represent complex and morally ambiguous positions. Blanche is far from perfect. She is a liar, an alcoholic, and she would break up the Kowalski marriage if she could. Despite his rough exterior, Stanley genuinely loves and needs his wife, and he cannot be blamed for protecting his marriage against the force that would destroy it. The ambiguity of Blanche and Stanley makes them more realistic than many of Williams's characters, who are often either demons (philistines with power, wealth, and influence) or angels (helpless, sensitive, down-trodden artists or women). Although Williams depicts both positive and negative personality traits in Blanche and Stanley, his attitude toward the two characters changes in the course of the play. In the beginning Williams clearly favors Stanley by emphasizing his wholesome natural traits, while dwelling on Blanche's artificiality. But such, we learn, are the deceptive appearances. The more Williams delves into Blanche's inner life and presents it on stage, the more sympathetic she becomes. Stanley's true nature also becomes apparent, in its negative effect upon her psyche, and, in the end, she is the undisputed moral victor.

Kazan's production deliberately emphasized Stanley's positive traits. In his notes on directing the play Kazan specifies that Blanche be presented as the "heavy" at the beginning of the play. Simultaneously, of course, Stanley is to evoke the audience's sympathy. Harold Clurman reports on this aspect of the original production: "Because the author does not preach about him but draws him without hate or ideological animus, the audience takes him at his face value. . . . For almost more than two-thirds of the play, therefore, the audience identifies itself with Stanley Kowalski. His low jeering is seconded by the audience's laughter, which seems to mock the feeble and hysterical decorativeness of the girl's behavior." Clurman, in going on to condemn the attempt to ingratiate Stanley with the audience, overlooks the dramatic value of making Stanley appealing initially. Stanley is, after all, not a monster. He bears remarkable resemblance to the kind of hero that Americans love, the hero of the westerns or the tough detective stories: the gruff masculine pragmatist who commands the adulation of women even as he scorns them for his male companions. That he is not as harmless, as "right" as he seems is precisely Williams's point. The play forces the members of the audience, as well as Blanche, to face "harsh reality," for they learn that what they instinctively admire and view as healthy is really a base egotistical force, destructive of what it cannot comprehend. The audience too moves from illusion to reality. The initial tendency is to resent Blanche and her airs, to applaud Stanley every time he "takes her down a peg." But slowly, as the veil of illusion lifts, both Stanley and Blanche are seen more clearly. Marlon Brando, who played Stanley in the Kazan production and in the movie, was an excellent choice for an appealing Stanley. Irwin Shaw commented on Brando's Broadway performance:

> He is so appealing in a direct, almost childlike way in the beginning and we have been so conditioned by the modern doctrine that what is natural is good, that we admire him and sympathize with him. Then, bit by bit, with a full account of what his good points really are, we come dimly to see that he is . . . brutish, destructive in his healthy egotism, dangerous, immoral, surviving.
>
> ("Masterpiece," *The New Republic,* December 22, 1947.)

It is the rape scene that finally reveals the true horror of Stanley. As Blanche is made to face unpleasant reality in this scene, so is the audience.

Williams remains as much as possible within the conventions of verisimilitude in using theatrical devices to reveal Blanche's distorted vision of reality. The audience is, however, aware that baths and light bulbs have a meaning for Blanche apart from their functional existence. The further Blanche retreats from reality, the more Williams distorts the surface realism of the play. The purpose of the transparent wall in scene 1 is not to reveal what is actually occurring in the alley, but to provide the necessary milieu for the defeat of illusion and to offer objective correlatives for Blanche's fears. Similarly, the subjective sounds enable the audience to share Blanche's past experiences and her present terrors.

In theme and technique *A Streetcar Named Desire* is, in the words of Henry Taylor, the play "toward which . . . all Williams's work has been heading." The characters of his early one-act plays, of *The Glass Menagerie* and of *A Streetcar Named Desire* who doggedly cling to an imaginative vision of what life ought to be, while resolutely ignoring what life is, are invested with a dignity denied those who accommodate themselves to imperfect existence. The theme of the necessity of illusions lends itself to theatricalist treatment, since the nonobjective world, which is far more important to Williams's characters than the objective one, must somehow be made tangible on stage. Williams's use of theatrical devices to objectify thoughts and feelings is much more sophisticated in *A Streetcar Named Desire* than in his hitherto most successful play, *The Glass Menagerie*. In the earlier play Williams thought he needed a screen to depict exact and obvious equivalents for his characters' thoughts. In *A Streetcar Named Desire* he relies more upon the suggestive qualities of costuming and staging to communicate psychological tendencies more subliminal than thought. *The Glass Menagerie*'s musical themes, particularly the sentimental fiddling and the jolly roger tune, reflect not so much the characters' inner lives, as the author's ironic perspective on them. On the other hand, in *A Streetcar Named Desire,* the nightclub music and the Varsouviana convey the emotional states of the characters at each stage of the action.

The realism of *A Streetcar Named Desire* distinguishes it from *Summer and Smoke* (written before, but produced after *Streetcar*), with which it is superficially related. In *Summer and Smoke* the conflict is between two abstractions; in *A Streetcar Named Desire,* it is between two people. The angel, anatomy chart, and divided stage of *Summer and Smoke* simplify Alma and John so that they represent abstract qualities. John, who represents first body and later soul, lacks the ambiguity that makes Stanley a good dramatic character and a worthy opponent for Blanche. Stanley is as much a bundle of contradictions as his antagonist. His strength, brutality, and virility are balanced by his vulnerability to Blanche's attacks, his awkward attempts at tenderness, and his need for his wife's approval. The unexpected character changes of *Summer and Smoke,* the "turnabouts" necessary to demonstrate the proposition that body and soul are irreconcilable, have no parallel in *A Streetcar Named Desire.* The only event of any significance in *Summer and Smoke,* Alma's transformation, is not depicted on stage; it occurs between the acts. By contrast, Blanche's gradual emotional collapse is presented stage by stage. When Williams can no longer convey the disintegration of her mind by depicting only objective reality, he resorts to distortion of verisimilitude in order to present subjective reality. Blanche does not mechanically move from one extreme to the other; she suffers and undergoes—on stage. The difference between *A Streetcar Named Desire* and *Summer and Smoke* is not, as an occasional critic has suggested, between a melodramatic and a "subtle" presentation of the same action, but between a play that finds adequate expression for the conflicts between and within individuals and one that sidesteps such conflicts completely.

Williams achieves his most successful revelation of human nature in its totality in this play in which he distorts the realistic surface as little as possible and only when necessary. The audience accepts as believable the direct depiction of Blanche's fantasies because the necessary touchstone in recognizable reality is consistently maintained. John Gassner writes: "The solution of the esthetic crisis in the theatre depends on our knowing when and how to combine the resources of realistic and theatricalist artistry" *(Directions in Modern Theatre and Drama).* *A Streetcar Named Desire* reveals an unerring sense of when and how to combine realism and theatricalism.

The Cards Indicate a Voyage on *A Streetcar Named Desire*

Leonard Quirino

> 'Art is made out of symbols the way your body is made out
>   of vital tissue.'
>
> TENNESSEE WILLIAMS

> ' "They are the souls," answered his [Aeneas'] father Anchises,
> "Whose destiny it is a second time
> To live in the flesh and there by the waters of Lethe
> They drink the draught that sets them free from care
> And blots out memory." '
>
> Description of the inhabitants of Elysian Fields
in Book 6 of the *Aeneid*

So much has been written about A *Streetcar Named Desire* in terms of its theatrical presentation as interpreted by a specific director and set of actors and so much concern has been lavished on the social attitudes and psychological constitution of its characters that the author's primary intention as revealed in his use of mythic symbolism and archetypal imagery to create a dialectic between soul and body to depict universally significant problems such as the conflict and mutual attraction between desire and death has been generally obscured or denigrated as pretentious. My own intention in this essay is to consider the play neither as interpreted in any specific production nor as it may embody a study of satyriasis, nymphomania, or reconstruction in the South, but, rather, as it constitutes what an examination of its symbolism reveals to be Tennessee Williams's intention:

From *Tennessee Williams: A Tribute,* edited by Jac Tharpe. © 1977 by the University Press of Mississippi.

a tragic parable dramatizing existence, the fact of incarnation, itself. Far from wishing to dissolve Williams's carefully constructed characters and theatrical effects into illustrations of archetypal figures or myths devoid of the author's particular "signature," I shall try to suggest how Williams's special use of two very ordinary symbols—the cards of destiny and the voyage of experience—aesthetically patterns the mosaic of his literary and theatrical imagery in *Streetcar,* investing the play with an artistry and meaning that transcend the mere theatricality and sensationalism with which it has so often been credited and discredited.

"Catch!" says Stanley Kowalski throwing a bloodstained package of meat to his wife, Stella, at the opening of the first scene of *A Streetcar Named Desire.* Laughing breathlessly, she manages to catch it. "This game is seven-card stud," reads the last line of the play. In between, much of the verbal and theatrical imagery that constitutes the drama is drawn from games, chance and luck. Williams had called the short play from which *Streetcar* evolved *The Poker Night,* and in the final version two of the most crucial scenes are presented within the framework of poker games played onstage. Indeed, the tactics and ceremonial of games in general, and poker in particular, may be seen as constituting the informing structural principle of the play as a whole. Pitting Stanley Kowalski, the powerful master of Elysian Fields against Blanche DuBois, the ineffectual ex-mistress of Belle Reve, Williams makes the former the inevitable winner of the game whose stakes are survival in the kind of world the play posits. For the first four of the eleven scenes of *Streetcar,* Blanche, by reason of her affectation of gentility and respectability, manages to bluff a good hand in her game with Stanley; thus, in the third scene Stanley is continually losing, principally to Mitch the potential ally of Blanche, in the poker game played onstage. However, generally suspicious of Blanche's behavior and her past, and made aware at the end of the fourth scene that she considers him an ape and a brute, Stanley pursues an investigation of the real identity of *her* cards. As, little by little, he finds proof of what he considers her own apishness and brutality, he continually discredits her gambits until, in the penultimate scene, he caps his winnings by raping her. In the last scene of the play, Stanley is not only winning every card game being played onstage, but he has also won the game he played with Blanche. Depending as it does on the skillful manipulation of the hands that chance deals out, the card game is used by Williams throughout *Streetcar* as a symbol of fate and of the skillful player's ability to make its decrees perform in his own favor at the expense of his opponent's misfortune, incompetence, and horror of the game itself.

Equally as important as the symbol of the card game in *Streetcar* is the imagery connected with the mythic archetype of the voyage which Williams portrays both as quest for an imagined ideal and as flight from disillusioning actuality."They told me," says Blanche in her first speech, "to take a streetcar named Desire, and then to transfer to one called Cemeteries and ride six blocks and get off at—Elysian Fields." Putting together the allergorical names of these streetcars and their destination at Elysian Fields with Williams's portrayal of Blanche as resembling a moth, traditionally a symbol of the soul, we find in her journey a not too deeply submerged metaphor for the soul's disastrous voyage through life. Caged in a body that it attempts to transcend but cannot escape, the moth-soul yearns for the star (Stella) and for rest in the isles of the happy dead; it finds, instead, the flaming "red hot" milieu of the primal blacksmith ("Stanley" or "stonelea" suggests the Stone Age man and "Kowalski" is Polish for "smith") and a world even more blatantly dedicated to "epic fornications" than its native Belle Reve, a world that shows every sign of prevailing. We are not surprised to learn that the agent of Blanche's journey to Elysian Fields, her school superintendent, is a Mr. Graves, and we can understand the implications of Blanche's statement late in the play, "The opposite [of death] is desire," to be more than merely sexual. Shuttling between yearning and frustration defines the basic rhythm of life itself for Blanche. Opening with her arrival in the land of life in death, the play chronicles the human soul's past and present excursions in the only vehicle that fate provides her, the rattle-trap streetcar of the body; the play closes with the soul's departure for incarceration in another asylum, another kind of living death.

Because the play, so rich in effects, is made to cohere largely by means of Williams's use of the imagery and symbolism of the voyage and the ceremonial and jargon of card games, a detailed exploration of *Streetcar* focusing on these two textural and structural principles might prove rewarding in assessing its artistic achievement. The ultimate aim of such an examination of the symbolism of the play, of course, is to demonstrate that the proper sphere of *Streetcar* is not the socio-clinical one to which it is so often relegated, but the realm of the tragic-universal which is more often than not denied it.

The epigraph to *A Streetcar Named Desire* is taken from Hart Crane's "The Broken Tower":

And so it was I entered the broken world
To trace the visionary company of love, its voice

> An instant in the wind (I know not whither hurled)
> But not for long to hold each desperate choice.

Besides focusing attention on Williams's positing of *two* broken worlds, both Belle Reve and Elysian Fields, and on the vision of life as a making of desperate choices, the epigraph introduces Williams's theme of the soul's quest for ideal love in the most unlikely of places—the broken world of actuality. Both the broken worlds which Williams compares and contrasts in the play bear wish-fulfilling names, but neither of these worlds fulfills Blanche's dreams of the ideal and of romantic love.

Blanche's first speech provides the introduction to Williams's treatment of her journey in the universal terms of life (desire) and death (cemeteries). In depicting her destination, Elysian Fields, which proves unwelcome and unwelcoming to Blanche, Williams continues to fuse and juxtapose images of life and death. In the ninth scene, for example, which takes place on the evening of Blanche's birthday (and shortly before the expected birth of the Kowalski child) a Mexican crone hawks "flores para los muertos" through the Elysian Fields offering her funeral "corones" to Blanche. In the previous scene, during the ghastly celebration of her own birthday, Blanche had been presented with a bus ticket back to Laurel (a name which ironically suggests wreaths of immortality) where she is even less welcome than she is in Stanley's domain. The birthday gift is a death sentence, and the soul on its desperate journey through existence finds destinations that are progressively horrifying. "Travelling," Blanche confesses, "wears me out."

Elysium, the paradise of the happy dead for the Greek poets, becomes in *Streetcar* a street which "runs between the L & N tracks and the river." Its flanks themselves suggest voyage although only the train ride, like the journey by streetcar, connotes horror for Blanche: "Out there I suppose is the ghoul-haunted woodland of Weir!" "No, honey," Stella replies, "those are the L and N tracks" (1,252). But for Blanche whose mental landscape is haunted by her dead husband, the allusion to Poe's "Ulalume" in which the memory of a dead love haunts the narrator of the poem is extremely appropriate. Although she is fearful of further locomotive journeys of desire, Blanche regards the prospect of voyage by water with pleasure. She dreams of cruising the Caribbean on a yacht with Shep Huntleigh (whose first name suggests a pastoral swain and whose last name suggests aristocratic sport) and, in the last scene, even looks forward to death on the sea: "I can smell the sea air. The rest of my time I'm going to spend on the sea. And when I die, I'm going to die on the sea."

Throughout the play, Blanche's addiction to water and to the baths which make her feel "Like a brand new human being," her hydrotherapy as she calls it, seems to be connected with the geography and function of the Elysian Fields as represented both in myth and in Williams's play.

In myth, the dead who entered the Elysian Fields were made to drink of the water of the river Lethe to forget all traces of their mortal past. And in book 6 of the *Aeneid,* Vergil depicts Lethe as a kind of watery purgatory where the dead are cleansed of all taint of memory and desire before they can be considered fit for reincarnation. In his adaptation of the concept of Elysian Fields for *Streetcar,* Williams, until the very end when he allows her the refuge of madness, denies the memory-haunted Blanche the full powers of the river Lethe. He depicts Stella, on the other hand, as one of the happy dead: after a night in bed with Stanley, "Her eyes and lips have that almost narcotized tranquility that is in the faces of Eastern idols." While Stella can bridge the two worlds of Belle Reve and Elysian Fields, Blanche is unwelcome in both.

This distinction is important to note because too many critics have made oversimplified, sociologically oriented interpretations of the conflict in *Streetcar* as a representation of Williams's nostalgia for vanished, decadent southern aristocracy and his horror of vital industrial proletarianism. Other critics, noticing that Williams *compares* as well as contrasts Belle Reve with Elysian Fields, claim that his presentation of social conditions is ambivalent and confusing. But Williams, usually little interested in sociology beyond its reflection of the human predicament of survival, does not use Blanche's pretentious cultural standards—which he exposes as pitiful—to measure Belle Reve against Elysian Fields; rather, he emphasizes the uninhabitability of both for his supremely romantic heroine to the extent that she symbolizes the soul. The vitality and "raffish charm" of Elysian Fields is outweighed by its brutality; the fabled graciousness of Belle Reve by its debauchery. The former world with its brawling, bowling cocks-of-the-walk is male-dominated; the latter as its grammatically incorrect name (feminine adjective modifying masculine noun) suggests is a female-oriented, effeminate world whose scions, as symbolized by Blanche's young husband, are apt to be disinclined to propagate. Blanche's remark to Stella about Stanley early in the play, "But maybe he's what we need to mix with our blood now that we've lost Belle Reve" proves, in the light of his (and even Mitch's) rough treatment of her, ironic. There can be no copulation or reconciliation between the world of the "beautiful dream" and the world of death in life actuality that will be mutually and ideally satisfactory. Stella's erotic will to life at any cost, her ability to shut one eye to the claims of the ideal and the other to the horrors of the actual, Williams portrays not as an easy truce between the two worlds but as a "narcotized," quasifatalistic commitment to survival that resolves none of the existential problems it poses.

Elysian Fields, the world that has replaced Belle Reve, will do, Williams seems to be saying, for the insensitive Stanley and the pragmatic Stella just as it provides satisfaction for their upstairs neighbors, the Hubbells, whom he names Eunice (literally "good victory") and Steve (literally "crown"); but it can only further the process of destroying Blanche which Belle Reve had begun. Its amusement-park thrills, its desperately gay and feverish music provide sufficient fulfilment only for the undemanding. The spirit of the whole place is characterized by the name of one of its nightspots, the "Four Deuces"—the poorest of the best hands in poker.

The introduction of Blanche's homosexual husband, Allan Grey, into the design of *Streetcar* has seemed gratuitously sensationalistic to some critics. Mary McCarthy, for example, found Blanche's story of the marriage so "patently untrue" that she took it upon herself to vouch for its incredibility to others: "the audience thinks the character must have invented it." Openly hostile to Williams's symbolism and incapable of interpreting it fairly (she insists on comparing Blanche to a typical sister-in-law —whatever that may be), Miss McCarthy failed to realize that Allan Grey, the deviate poet of Laurel and Belle Reve, is presented as the extreme opposite of the "gaudy seed-bearer" of Elysian Fields, that Blanche's attraction to him is as credible as is her abhorrence for Stanley, and that Blanche's relationship with her young husband proves mutually destructive because Williams's intention was to portray the impossibility of ideally consummating any union in which the body is involved. In Blanche's marriage Williams portrayed the futility of the romantic preoccupation with trying to achieve fulfilment with an epipsychidion or soul mate; in Blanche's intimacies with strangers and with Stanley he portrays the alternative to, and dramatizes the consequences of, that futile quest for fulfilment. "After the death of Allan—," Blanche tells Mitch, "intimacies with strangers was all I seemed able to fill my empty heart with. . . . I think it was panic, just panic, that drove me from one to another, hunting for some protection—here and there, in the most—unlikely places—even, at last, in a seventeen-year-old boy." Throughout the play we are aware of Blanche's being ghoul-haunted by the suicide of her husband and we witness her interlude with the young newsboy whom she envisions as a prince out of the Arabian Nights. Her last attempt to settle for rest with Mitch is thwarted: she has misjudged even that simple soul and is denied even the small demands she makes of this love. All her intimacies have been with strangers to her deepest yearnings. Only when we realize this can be fully appreciate the irony, pathos, and horror of her last line in the play: "Whoever you are—I have always depended on the kindness of strangers."

There can be salvation for Blanche neither in the pretentious world of Bella Reve from which she has salvaged only a trunk full of artificial goods and a head full of nightmares nor in the sex-glutted death in life of Elysian Fields because in *Streetcar* Williams has devised a conflict for her which only annihilation can resolve. As a symbol of the soul pitted against and in thrall to the body which fetters it, her natural state, like the moth's, is frustrating.

In the fourth scene of *Streetcar,* the following colloquy takes place between Stella and Blanche about the satisfactions of the flesh:

> STELLA: But there are things that happen between a man and a woman in the dark—that sort of make everything else seem—unimportant.
> BLANCHE: What you are talking about is brutal desire—just— Desire!—the name of that rattle-trap streetcar that bangs through the Quarter, up one old narrow street and down another . . .
> STELLA: Haven't you every ridden on that streetcar?
> BLANCHE: It brought me here.—Where I'm not wanted and where I'm ashamed to be.

The banging of the tired old streetcar up and down the narrow streets simulates Blanche's view of intercourse just as, in the very first scene, Stella's breathless laughter upon catching the bloodstained package of meat that Stanley throws her simulates *her* reaction to sexuality. In neither case does Williams portray sexuality, which he views as part of a cruel life force, in an attractive light. When Blanche says of Desire, "It brought me here" we may take her to mean not only the streetcar that bore her to Elysian Fields, the land of the living dead, but human desire which brought her into existence. Incarnation is what she is ashamed of, and the flesh is what she has abused in her self-punishment for submitting to its importunate demands. "A man like that is someone to go out with," she tells Stella, "—once—twice—three times when the devil is in you. But live with? Have a child by?" Blanche has been conditioned to believe that the anarchy of the flesh must, whenever possible, be transcended in the interests of family and culture; Williams, however, dramatizes the futility of attempts to transcend the limitations of the human animal.

At the end of this fourth scene, imploring Stella to leave Stanley, Blanche delivers a harangue which in its cadence and hysterical rhetoric betrays her desperation and vulnerability. Describing Stanley as the amoral mortal enemy of humanistic aspiration, she says: "He acts like an animal, has an animal's habits! . . . Thousands and thousands of years have passed him right by, and there he is—Stanley Kowalski—survivor of the Stone Age! Bearing the raw meat home from the kill in the jungle! . . . Night falls and the other apes gather! . . . His poker night!—you call it—this party of apes! . . . Maybe we are a long way from being made in God's image, but Stella—my sister—there has been *some* progress since then! Such things as art—as poetry and music—such kinds of new light have come into the world since then! In some kinds of people some tenderer feelings have had some little beginning! That we have got to make *grow*! and *cling* to, and hold as our flag! In this dark march toward whatever it is we're approaching. . . . *Don't—don't hang back with the brutes!*" Williams frames this speech, just before it begins and immediately after it ends, with the sound of two trains running like the old rattle-trap of Desire: at the same time, he has Stanley enter, unheard because of the noise of the trains, and remain to listen unobserved to Blanche's speech. Her two destroyers, desire and Stanley Kowalski, are thus made to hover like fateful accomplices over Blanche as she implores Stella to join with her in battle against them. That Stanley is placed in the strategically superior position of the unobserved viewer of the scene forecasts his eventual triumph over Blanche. To emphasize the inefficacy of Blanche's appeal and struggle against her fate, Williams ends the scene with Stella's embracing Stanley "fiercely"—joining the "brutes"—as Stanley grins at Blanche in victory. From that point on, Stanley begins to gain the upper hand in the struggle with Blanche.

Though in her long speech Blanche, characteristically rhapsodic, views the main struggle of existence as one between culture and brutality, the context of the play provides the struggle with wider, metaphysical significance. As a soul subjected to existence and hence to a body, her quarrel is not only with apes and brutes but with the apishness and brutality of matter with which she herself is involved and by which her mothlike flightiness is crippled and doomed. She herself has been unable to resist brutal treatment of her husband and she herself has ridden, without discernible satisfaction, on the streetcar of desire whose tracks, unlike the rungs of Plato's ladder of love, pointed to no great destination. Quite the contrary, for Blanche the desire and pursuit of the whole has proved, in practice, to lead to further disintegration.

While Stella and even Stanley would not, by any theological standards, be considered devoid of a soul, Williams prefers to dramatize the soulfulness of Blanche at their expense because he conceives of the soul not in dogmatically theological but in ideal terms. For Williams, the soul appears to be that impulse in humanity which aspires to transcend the natural corruption and propensity to declivity that he constantly portrays as the informing principle of matter. Whereas he presents Stella and the earthy Stanley as the living dead narcotized by sex, gaming and comic books, characters contentedly buried in what Strindberg in *The Ghost Sonata* called "the dirt of life," Williams portrays Blanche as guiltily drawn to water and baths and as claiming, preciously, that she would die of eating an unwashed grape. The soul, for Williams in this play, seems to be that entity which produces and is sustained by culture but is not synonymous with it. It is that entity which, desiring the Good, is yet powerless to attain it by reason of the inexorable baseness of the matter that incarnates it. When Stanley, overpowering Blanche at the climax of the play says, "We've had this date with each other from the beginning," Williams is portraying what he views as the fated culmination of the soul's struggle against the body. The words "from the beginning"—in the mythic context of the drama—suggest the origins of the human race itself. All of Blanche's mothlike rushing and dashing about, which the stage directions call for her to do, cannot save her from the flame with which she has flirted. Though she was able to frighten Mitch away by shouting "Fire!" she collapses when faced with this more powerful flame to which her treacherous body draws her.

The predominating conflict of flesh and spirit modifies and includes all the other conflicts—sociological, psychological, moral, cultural—which *A Streetcar Named Desire* presents. It would be an oversimplification, as I have stated above, to see Belle Reve and Elysian Fields merely as opposites when Williams has subtly pointed out their similarity and the shortcomings they share in fulfilling the claims of the ideal. And it would be simpleminded to call Williams's presentation of both the attractiveness and failure of these two ways of life as ambivalence and to claim that it mars the play. By pitting the sterility of Belle Reve against the fertility of Elysian Fields, the weakness of Blanche against the insensitive stolidity of Stanley, her cultural pretensions against his penis-status, her sorority-girl vision of courtship and good times against his "colored-lights" orgasms, the simulated pearls of her lies against the swinish truth of his facts, her uncontrollable epic fornications against Stanley's own, less hysterical mastery in this area of experience, Williams attempts to dramatize the inevitable succumbing of the former to the greater power of the latter. If he seems to favor Blanche, it is because she is the weaker and because, at one time, as Stella attests, she showed great potential for tenderness and trust, the qualities of a typical victim. Only her stifled potential and her futile aspirations to transcend or mitigate the harshness of actuality—to cover the naked light bulb with a paper lantern—seem to qualify her, in Williams's eyes, as a symbol of the trapped soul. Not even her moral code, "Deliberate cruelty . . . is the one unforgivable thing . . . the one thing of which I have never, never been guilty," admirable as far as it goes, qualifies her as a symbol of transcendence so much as her pitiful attempts to combat actuality do. And, ironically and tragically enough, it is her very preference for soulful illusion and for magic over actuality which paves the way for her voyage to the madhouse.

Aware of the pity and terror of Blanche's world, Williams is not blind to the same qualities in the world that abides by Stanley's "Napoleonic Code." Stella and Mitch, for example, as creatures less hard than Stanley must nevertheless abide by his rules and even his lies (such as his denial of raping Blanche) if they are to survive in his domain. Though the furies of retribution visit Blanche for her hubris in making too many impossible demands of the "broken world" of mortality, they do not seem powerful enough to affect her antgonist, Stanley. In a way, the plot of *Streetcar* is modeled on the legend of Tereus, Philomela and Procne—the rape of the visiting sister-in-law by her brother-in-law in the absence of his wife—but Blanche's sister does not cut up her baby and serve it to Stanley for dinner as Procne served her son to Tereus; instead, Stella refuses to believe the story of the rape in order to go on living with Stanley and to provide a home for their child. Nor do the gods enter and transform the triangle into a trio of birds. And, while Mitch appears to believe that Stanley raped Blanche, he is powerless to overthrow his old master sergeant whose code of morality he must continue to endure just as, in the past, he was influenced by it in his treatment of Blanche.

While Williams dramatizes the plight of the incarnated, incarcerated soul primarily in terms of her futile voyage in quest of fulfillment—or, failing that, of peace and rest—he portrays the roles that fate and luck play in existence primarily in images of gaming. And the master of games in *Streetcar* is Stanley Kowalski. By reason of his amoral fitness for survival in a world which, in Williams's Darwinian view, is geared to the physically strongest at the expense of the meekly vulnerable, Stanley has an "in" with the fates. Though the intrusion of Blanche into his world rattles Stanley and threatens to undermine the self-confidence that sustains his power, he systematically allays his own fears at the expense of aggravating Blanche's. Though he loses at the poker games played in scene three, he wins at those played in the last scene of the play.

Introducing fate into his play by way of luck at games, Williams pits Stanley's chances of survival against Blanche's. When Williams summed up the moral of the play as, "If we don't watch out, the apes will take over," he expressed the same view of existence that he delegated to Blanche in her speech denouncing the poker players as "a party of apes." That the tone and strategy of the play reveal it not merely as a cautionary drama but as a tragedy of the futility of attempting to flee the apes, I have stressed above. What the play really demonstrates is that, willy-nilly, the apes *must* take over since apishness is presented throughout as the natural, unavoidable condition not only of survival but of existence itself. A close examination of the Poker Night scene displays Williams's remarkable use of mythic and symbolic imagery to orchestrate both the "moral" of the play as he is reported to see it and the wider context in which I have been placing it.

Williams describes the poker players in scene 3, Stanley, Steve, Pablo and Mitch, as "men at the peak of their physical manhood, as coarse and direct and powerful as the primary colors" of the kitchen setting. As the scene opens, Stanley is losing and Mitch, who is shortly to meet Blanche, has been winning and is no longer in the game. They have apparently been playing games in which specific cards are "wild," games that depend to a greater extent on luck (read "fate") than on skill. In the game which we witness, "One-eyed jacks are wild." The rule of this game seems to describe the wild players themselves both as knaves and, in the mythic context of the play, as Cyclopes who, like these players, dwelt apart in caverns, observed no social, moral or legal order and existed by advantage of rude, savage strength unhampered by culture or intellect. By the end of the scene, we will be made witness to their apishness, particularly Stanley's (who as "Kowalski" is linked metaphorically with the Cyclopes who worked as smiths for Vulcan), and we will observe in action the caveman attraction he exerts for Stella whom he carries off to bed with him in their flat which is described as cavelike in the stage directions. Much is made, at the opening of the scene, of Mitch as a mamma's boy. He is playing in a game whose ultimate victors will not be the gentler giants attached to mothers, dead financées and flighty moths, but the rougher giants who survive and prevail by means of their brutishness and sheer brag.

The symbolic name of the second game played in this scene, "seven-card stud," is, of course, obvious in the context of these Elysian Fields where values are based on studmanship. While the cards for this game are being dealt out, Steve tells a joke about hens and roosters: the animalistic view of existence is underlined to contrast with Blanche's unsuccessfully transcendental one. As the joke ends, Blanche and Stella, the hens of the household, appear. They are unwelcome intruders in the masculine game. The scene then continues in twin focus on the card game in the kitchen and on Blanche's flirtation with Mitch in the bedroom.

Immediately before Blanche's first conversation with Mitch, Stanley had decided to play "Spit in the Ocean," a game which demands the pushing of one's luck. The name of the game suggests Stanley's attitude to Blanche's dream of ocean voyage and her addiction to the purgative and healing functions of water and, in line with the mythic context of the play, recalls the ancient superstition, popular with the Greeks and Romans, of spitting in the ocean to ward off enchantment and enchanters. The game played by Stanley in the kitchen provides an aptly ironic accompaniment to the game Blanche plays in the bedroom where, in her red satin wrapper, she flirts with Mitch, smokes his "Luckies," has him put up her paper lantern, dances to the music of a Viennese waltz, and tries to create the kind of "enchantment" that is unwelcome in Stanley's world. The romantic bedroom scene is abruptly terminated with Stanley's going as wild as a one-eyed Jack, or Cyclops, breaking the radio, striking Stella, and battling the other apes. Stanley's destructiveness, which Stella fondly rationalizes in the next scene as part of his passionate nature, is also part of the gaudy seed-bearer's physical potency. It is described by Blanche as "lunacy" but Williams ironically emphasizes its normalcy in context of the view of nature he presents in the play, and he has Blanche, instead, carted off as a lunatic at the end.

The Poker Night scene ends when Stella, unable to resist Stanley's "howling," "baying" and "bellowing" for her, returns to him: "they come together with low, animal moans. . . . [Stanley] lifts her off her feet and bears her into the dark flat." Outside the apartment, terrified, Blanche flits and rushes about like a moth looking "right and left as if for a sanctuary." She is calmed and comforted by Mitch.

Throughout the play, images drawn from gaming, chance and luck compete in number with those suggesting water and voyage. The sixth scene, for example, renders Mitch's marrige proposal to Blanche within the framework of imagery suggesting the game of chance which Blanche is desperately playing with him and with survival. The scene opens with the return home of Blanche and Mitch from their unsatisfactory date. "They have probably," the stage directions tell us, "been out to the amusement park on Lake Pontchartrain, for Mitch is bearing, upside down, a plaster statuette of Mae West, the sort of prize won at shooting galleries and carnival games of chance." At the door to Stanley's flat, Blanche says, "I'm looking for the Pleiades, the Seven Sisters, but these girls are not out tonight. Oh, yes they are, there they are! God bless them! All in a bunch going home from their little bridge party." The presence of the Pleiades in the sky seems to comfort Blanche; her reference to them as bridge ladies not only aligns them with the imagery of existence as a game of chance, but the familiarity with which Blanche treats the seven nymphs who, even as stars, must constantly flee the mighty, devastating hunter, Orion, suggests mythically and cosmically, a parallel to her own danger, pursued as she is by Stanley's vital lust for domination and destruction. The scene ends with Blanche's pathetic belief that Mitch's proposal is a sign that the gods have furnished her with an earthly protector. "Sometimes—," she says, "there's God—so quickly!" The name "Mitch" or "Mitchell," incidentally, is derived from "Michael" and means "someone like God," but the godlike figure in this play is shown to be less powerful than—indeed in thrall to—the primal savage force represented by Stanley.

Generally, the two major image patterns concerned with voyage (particularly as escape from fate by means of water) and with games (as the framework of human chance and destiny) are only very casually suggested; occasionally they are even joined in a single speech as when Blanche, for example, explains to Mitch why she has come to Elysian Fields: "There was nowhere else I could go, I was *played out.* You know what played out is? My youth was suddenly gone up the *water-spout,* and—I met you . . ." (italics mine). In the last scene of the play, Williams more forcefully calls attention to his two most important image patterns in a superbly executed finale that boldly juxtaposes them.

Scene 11 opens with these two stage directions:

> *It is some weeks later. Stella is packing Blanche's things. Sound of water can be heard running in the bathroom.*

The portieres are partly open on the poker players—Stanley, Steve, Mitch and Pablo—who sit around the table in the kitchen. The atmosphere of the kitchen is now the same raw, lurid one of the disastrous poker night." The first words of dialogue in this scene are spoken by Stanley, the ultimate victor in the game between flesh and spirit: "Drew to an inside straight and made it, by God." *"Maldita sea tu suerto!"* says Pablo. Stanley, accustomed to winning by taking unfair advantage of whoever is weaker or of what he cannot understand, says, "Put it in English, greaseball." During the play, Stanley himself has been described in the stage directions as "grease-stained" and even by Stella as "greasy"; now, however, as the vanquisher of Blanche, he lords it over the socially inferior, Spanish-speaking Pablo just as, previously, Blanche and Stella, "a pair of queens," had condescended to him, "I am cursing your rutting luck," says Pablo, whose choice of epithet aptly describes the reason for Stanley's power in the Elysian Fields, his fabulous rutting. Stanley, "prodigiously elated," then explains his view of luck: "You know what luck is? Luck is believing you're lucky. Take at Salerno. I believed I was lucky. I figured that 4 out of 5 would not come through but I would . . . and I did. I put that down as a rule. To hold front position in this rat-race you've got to believe you are lucky." The combination of physical and sexual potency together with his knowledge of the odds and his capacity for thinking positively assures Stanley, as Williams pictures him, survival in any war or race, human or rat. Mitch, unable to countenance Stanley's self-assurance, blurts out: "You . . . you . . . you . . . Brag . . . brag . . . bull . . . bull." Even apart from the way Mitch apparently means the terms "brag" and "bull" here, he is appropriately summarizing Stanley's major claims to success. As a noun, *brag* is the name of a card game in which the players *brag* about holding cards better than those that have been dealt them. And *bull,* of course, suggests the awesome fertility that is geared to the successful cowing of other players in any game of seven-card stud.

After introducing the theme of the fatal card game as an analogue of earthly existence, the last scene of *Streetcar* shifts to focus on Eunice and Stella as they prepare Blanche for another journey. Speaking from the bathroom which has been her refuge throughout the play, Blanche asks, "Is the coast clear?" As Eunice and Stella assist her to dress, Blanche treats them like two handmaidens preparing her for a romantic ocean voyage. With "faintly hysterical vivacity" she concerns himself with her clothes and appearance. In having Blanche ask for a bunch of artificial violets to be pinned with a seahorse on the lapel of her jacket, Williams portrays her insignia: the violet which traditionally symbolizes innocence in flower language together with the creature whose natural habitat would be water— not land.

When Blanche meets the doctor who has come for her and sees that he is not Shep Huntleigh, the stage directions read, "There is a moment of silence—no sound but that of Stanley steadily shuffling the cards." As Blanche tries to escape the doctor, "The Matron advances on one side, Stanley on the other. Divested of all the softer properties of womanhood, the Matron is a peculiarly sinister figure in her severe dress. Her voice is bold and toneless as a firebell." When the matron says, "Hello, Blanche," "The greeting is echoed and reechoed by other mysterious voices behind the walls, as if reverberated through a canyon of rock." The cold, peculiarly sinister figure of the matron whose firebell voice subsumes and awakens echoes of the other voices which have haunted Blanche in the play may be seen as the archetypal embodiment of disaster for her. When Williams states that the matron's greeting must sound like the reverberations in a canyon, we are reminded of Blanche's speech to Mitch about being "played out" which I quoted above and which introduces the image of the world as a rock: "I thanked God for you, because you seemed to be gentle—*a cleft in the rock of the world that I could hide in!*" (italics mine). However, Blanche's journey has provided her no canyon to hide in and now the hoped-for canyon itself is portrayed as reverberating with inescapable memories of horror. The theatrical image presented by Blanche's "retreating in panic" from the matron on the one hand and Stanley on the other suggests, in the mythic context of the play, the moth-soul trying to evade the grasp both of cold, earthy, mother-figure (portrayed in imagery that suggests a harsh view of mother nature herself) and that figure's ally described earlier in the play as a type of "gaudy seed-bearer." Blanche's two antagonists here form a theatrical icon of incarnation and existence that graphically summarizes the wider significance of her plight throughout the play.

Only when the old doctor becomes courtly and addresses Blanche gently does her panic abate and does she allow herself to be escorted from Elysian Fields. Blanche's last speech about her continual dependence on the kindess of strangers, though terrifying in context of what these strangers have subjected her to, allows her the dignity of repudiating, by implication, what her relations have done to her. At the same time, since the audience knows that Blanche is being conducted to the madhouse and, possibly, to her death there, the dignity of her repudiation is gained at the expense of the so-called sanity and brutal vitality of Elysian Fields, the Darwinian state of existence.

As Blanche leaves the scene, Eunice places Stanley's infant son in Stella's arms. Again, the images of destruction and creation are juxtaposed. Stella is sobbing and Stanley comforts her in the only way he knows how: "He kneels beside her and his fingers find the opening of her blouse." Echoing the sinister matron's attempts to subdue Blanche with the words, "Now, Blanche!" Stanley "voluptuously, soothingly" consoles Stella with "Now, honey. Now, love. Now, now, love. . . ." The play ends with the "swelling music of the 'blue piano' and the muted trumpet" as Steve says, "This game is seven-card stud."

Throughout *A Streetcar Named Desire,* Williams used every device of theatrical rhetoric to portray and orchestrate existence as a stud game. From the desperate gaiety of the tinny "Blue Piano" which Williams says in his first stage direction "expresses the spirit of the life which goes on here" to the brawling of the Kowalskis and their neighbors, from the cries of the street vendors ("Red hot!" and "Flores para los muertos") to what Elia Kazan called the "ballet" of the passerby in quest of money or sex, Williams created in *Streetcar* a frenetic dramatization of spiritual frustration and physical satiation alike, of life fraught with death (Blanche) and of death burning with life (Elysian Fields). Though not without its quieter moments and lyrical interludes, the play might best be characterized as a syncopated rendition of what Williams views as the basic rhythm of physical existence: tumescence and detumescence, desire and death.

While Williams appears to be primarily concerned with sexuality in *Streetcar,* his symbolic depiction of desire transcends merely sexual passion to include existence itself as its ultimate referent. One need not necessarily accept Freud's theory of the libido as the basic life force to appreciate what Williams means by equating, as Blanche does, desire with life. With more restraint than Williams in *Streetcar,* Paul Valéry in an essay on Flaubert makes much the same equation of desire (and frustration) with life that Williams dramatizes in the play. Variously calling desire "greed," "temptation" and "lack," Valéry writes: "In Nature the root of the tree pushes towards wet ground, the summit towards the sun, and the plant thrives by changing unbalance into unbalance, greed into greed. The amoeba deforms itself in approaching its tiny prey, obeys that which it is going to convert into its own substance, then hauls itself to its adventuring pseudopodium and reassembles itself. This type of mechanism is characteristic of all organic life; the devi, alas! is nature itself, and temptation is the most obvious, the most constant, the most inescapable condition of life. To live means to lack something at every moment—to modify oneself in order to attain it—and hence to aim at returning again to the state of lacking something." ("The Temptation of [Saint] Flaubert") It is on this basis that Williams identifies desire with the nature of existence itself and on this basis that he constrasts Blanche's continuous frustration with the narcotized, makeshift fulfilment that prevails in the Elysian Fields of the play.

To point out the symbolic, mythic and tragic implications of the literary and theatrical imagery in *Streetcar* is not to deny that the play is often as jazzy and comic as the vision of existence it depicts (though close inspection reveals that the jazz is usually desperate and the comedy often very cruel). Elements of melodrama, frequently present in tragedy, are also evident in its structure—to such an extent that they have sometimes blinded viewers to its other qualities. Even the usually perspicacious Susan Sontag wrote in her controversial essay of 1964, "Against Interpretation," that *Streetcar* should be enjoyed merely as "a forceful psychological melodrama . . . about a handsome brute named Stanley Kowalski and a faded mangy belle named Blanche DuBois . . ." and that any *other* interpretation of the play would be unwarranted.

What I have tried to do in this essay, however, is to avoid rehashing the most blatantly realistic aspects of the play and to view it, instead, in terms of Williams's persistent concern with creating universal and "timeless" worlds in his plays. In play after play, Williams has consistently (albeit with varying degrees of success) employed symbolism and the mythic mode to universalize the significance of the realistic action he posits, not only, apparently, because he thinks of symbolism and universality as essentials of art, but also because these qualities seem to be characteristic of his personal reactions to life in general. For example, speaking years later of the autobiographical genesis of *Streetcar,* Williams said that whenever he stayed in New Orleans, he lived "near the main street of the [French] Quarter which is named Royal. Down this street, running on the same tracks, are two street-cars, one named DESIRE and the other CEMETERY. Their indiscourageable progress up and down Royal struck me as having some symbolic bearing of a broad nature on the life in the *Vieux Carré*— and everywhere else for that matter."

Read in the light of Williams's personal and aesthetic predilections, all the images, symbols and allusions, even what appear to be only the most casual or realistic of details in *Streetcar,* combine to reveal a tragic parable of the pitiable and terrible fate of the human soul. Incarnated in treacherous, decaying matter, the soul, it appears, has been destined to voyage continually from one broken world to another, the only kinds of environment open to it in a flawed universe. Seeking union with the stars (themselves, whether symbolized as Stella or the Pleiades, in a precarious situation), or, failing that, at least repose in the extinction of memory and cares in the Elysian Fields, the moth-soul finds, instead, only another broken world, another Darwinian environment in which the brutally fittest rule. As Tennessee Williams dramatizes his vision of existence in *A Streetcar Named Desire,* we see that "from the beginning" the cards of destiny have indicated a seemingly endless voyage for the human soul through progressively disastrous worlds, and the name of the game is tragedy.

Drama of Intimacy and Tragedy of Incomprehension: *A Streetcar Named Desire* Reconsidered

Bert Cardullo

Much of the criticism of Tennessee Williams's *A Streetcar Named Desire* seems to me to miss the point in speaking unqualifiedly of Stanley Kowalski as the destroyer of Blanche DuBois. Harold Clurman, in what otherwise has to be one of the most perceptive commentaries on the play and its original Broadway production, writes misleadingly of a Stanley who, "drunk the night of his wife's labor, . . . *settles his account* [italics mine] with Blanche by raping her," and of a Blanche who "is ordered out of Stella's house." John Gassner, insisting on applying the terms of Aristotelian tragedy to *Streetcar* from without and seeing how well it conforms to them, instead of judging the play on its own terms with their specific implications, concludes that Stanley is a "brutal executioner [who] performs the act of destruction that Blanche *should have* [italics mine] performed for herself, having had within her the seeds of her own destruction." The list goes on and on, from Nancy Tischler's "moth beauty" of Blanche destroyed by the "brute ugliness" of Stanley to Jordan Y. Miller's and Signi Falk's bestial Stanley using the "ultimate weapon," rape, to take out his "revenge" on the sensitive Blanche.

Stanley Kowalski may perform the act which seals Blanche DuBois's doom once and for all, but, clearly, he has not consciously plotted to destroy her throughout the play. Convinced that Blanche was not a heroine of tragic proportions, critics over the years have looked outside what they have concluded to be a hopelessly demented character to find the agent of

---

her destruction and, quite naturally, come up with an evil, scheming Stanley. But Stella's husband is never so much maliciously intent on destroying his sister-in-law as he is blind to her problems and needs—a "tragedy
of incomprehension" Williams has called this play—however much
"truth" he uncovers abut her past, however much he reveals her talk to
be, in his words, only "imagination . . . and lies and conceit and tricks."
Blanche's struggle throughout *Streetcar* is surely more with herself than
with Stanley. Her *conflict* with him may be inevitable from the moment
she enters his home, given their opposing views of life and each's claim to
Stella. The inevitability of her doom, however, springs not from the character of this conflict but from her rejection of Allan Grey on the dance
floor of Moon Lake Casino many years before. Stanley's rape of Blanche
thus comes to appear the ironic physical incarnation of a defeat whose
seeds she herself inadvertently cultivated with "intimacies with strangers"
after her young husband's suicide, unable or unwilling to seek consolation,
"protection," elsewhere. Such rape must not be defined categorically as his
vengeful victory in the struggle to keep her from ruining his marriage and
altering or unsettling his way of life.

Indeed, Williams carefully structures act 3, scene 4, so as to make the
rape seem incidental, the result more of Stanley's sudden and uncontrollable drunken lust than of his calculation and deliberate cruelty. Stanley does
not rape Blanche because he knows her nervous breakdown and expulsion
from his home will result. Rather, he does so because he has been physically attracted to her from the start and has been encouraged by her on at
least one occasion, and is able to fuel his desires with knowledge of her
checkered past in Laurel. Too, he has probably not been sexually gratified
for some time due to his wife's growing pregnancy and the concurrent
dearth of privacy created by his sister-in-law's visit to their already
cramped quarters. Stanley has no reason to believe his act will have any
negative consequences, either for his marriage or for Blanche's state of
mind, since he presumes she will be leaving New Orleans by bus for Laurel on the following Tuesday and since he believes this is what she really
wants and is in fact accustomed to getting. When he says, "What are you
putting on now?" at the end of the scene, he means exactly what he says,
thinking Blanche's hysteria is merely an exaggerated reaction to his having
trapped her in a lie. (Significantly, Stanley never bothers to ask her *why*
she lied, or, for that matter, why she spoke out against him in the first
place at the end of act 1, scene 4. He is interested, has and could only have
been interested all along, in maintaining or reveling in his intimacy with
Stella, not in questioning Blanche's motives or defending his way of life

against hers.) And when he follows with, "Oh! So you want some rough-house!" he is reacting playfully to what he considers her momentary and obligatory, extravagantly affected resistance to his advances.

Stanley may feel avenged on Blanche as the *result* of the rape, but its *cause* is not his desire to avenge himself on her. Besides, he *has* his "revenge" on Blanche before entering the bathroom in this scene. Having caught her in the lie about the telegram from Shep Huntleigh, Stanley proceeds, in a large expenditure of energy, to condemn her for the "pack of lies" she has told over the past few months. He then signals his victory of *exposure* with a climactic explosion of ha-ha's. That is why the rape appears so incidental, so *anti*climactic. Stanley comes out of the bathroom at a level of relatively low energy and, blind to Blanche's dilemma, grins playfully as he seizes upon *her* demand that he let her get by him. Standing between Blanche and the door to his apartment, he then seizes upon his own laughing dismissal of *her* fear of interference to utter softly, haltingly, "Come to think of it—maybe you wouldn't be bad to—interfere with. . . ." His language from this point on is controlled and sometimes implicitly sexual, never angry and overtly revengeful. And it is certainly not unreasonable to assume that, were Stanley bent on revenge, he would characteristically browbeat Blanche into bed in a fierce struggle. Instead, Williams has *Blanche* threaten *Stanley* with the broken end of a beer bottle and him disarm her alertly before carrying her "inert figure" to bed. Her role as the passive victim of an act of incidental, *inadvertent* cruelty, of sudden lust and immediate "fun" or "diversion," is thus emphasized. Here the active resister of a premeditated, intentionally cruel act of revenge she is not.

As I have observed, those critics of *Streetcar* who dismiss the play outright as tragedy point to the character of Blanche as indisputably that of a clinical case history; they claim that the collapse of her marriage and the death of her homosexual husband made her a victim of neurosis. But they fail to take into account, in Leonard Berkman's words, that "Blanche's most fundamental regret is not that she happened to marry a homosexual," not the *discovery* of Allan's homosexuality (*Stella* believes this). It is that, "when made aware of her husband's homosexuality, she brought on [his] suicide by her unqualified expression of disgust," her *failure* to be compassionate. Confronted in theory with the choice between the expression of compassion and the expression of disgust at the sudden and stunning revelation of Allan's longstanding affair with an older man, she at first "pretended that nothing had been discovered." Then, unable to stop herself, she blurted out abruptly the words of contempt that drove her first and only love to kill himself. I say "confronted in theory with the choice" because, as Blanche herself confesses to Mitch, "[Allan] came to me for help. I didn't know that. . . . All I knew was I'd failed him in some mysterious way and wasn't able to give the help he needed but couldn't speak of! . . . I loved him unendurably but without being able to help him or help myself." Blanche could hardly be expected to respond with love and understanding to her discovery, "in the worst of all possible ways," of Allan's homosexuality (though she struggles to—that is one reason she does not express her disgust immediately), because she had never had a truly intimate, an open and trusting, relationship with him. In the same way, Williams leads us to believe she had never had such a relationship with any of her relatives at Belle Reve either, nor they with one another, as the DuBois men gradually exchanged the land for their "epic fornications" and the women dared not admit they had ever heard of death.

The evidence in the present for this conclusion is her relationship with Stella—hardly what could be called one of confidence and intimacy, despite the genuine feeling the sisters have for each other. As Blanche dreams airily in act 1 of Shep Huntleigh's block-long Cadillac convertible and a shop for *both* of them, Stella straightens up her apartment matter of factly and responds to her sister practically, if lightly, even disinterestedly. When Blanche cries out in desperation that she has left only "sixty-five measly cents in coin of the realm," Stella answers this veiled plea for rescue from a life bereft of warmth and affection with little more than an offer of five dollars and a Bromo and the suggestion that she "just let things go, at least for a—while." Stella, out of an overwhelming desire to negate her past and Blanche with it, or out of sheer self-indulgence, will, *can,* concern herself with nothing but the mindless and easy, sensuous pursuit of day-to-day living. When Blanche opens up to her in act 2 and speaks of "soft people" and "fading," Stella can only reject what she calls morbidity and offer her sister a Coke, even as she offered to pour the drinks in act 1, scene 1. And when at the end of act 3, scene 1, Blanche wants to know what has happened, Stella is unable to confront her with what Stanley has reported, even as Blanche herself was unable to confront Allan with what she had discovered until it was too late. In a stunning unmasking of character toward the end of the same scene, Stella reacts to Stanley's purchase of the bus ticket with, "In the first place, Blanche wouldn't go on a bus." She objects to the *means* of transportation instead of expressing immediate incredulity, outrage and dismay at the *idea* of sending her sister away.

Blanche is closer to tragic heroine than many would like to think, then, "in [her] refusal to shirk a responsibility that the conventional society of her time and place would have eagerly excused . . . ," to quote Leonard Berkman. She refuses from the beginning to forgive herself for denying Allan the compassion that would have saved and perhaps changed him, or at any rate made his burden easier to bear. She struggles at the end in his memory to achieve intimacy with Mitch—the ony true intimacy within her grasp—which alone can restore her to grace through its inherent linking of sex with compassion. It is thus not arbitrarily or gratuitously, or simply out of her own pure joy, that Williams has Blanche declare, "Sometimes—there's God—so quickly!" at the end of act 2, scene 2. Rather, he has her so reenter a state of grace as a direct result of the embrace and kiss she exchanges with Mitch, of their recognition, finally, of a real need and desire for one another. In this light, the "intimacies with strangers," the sex *without* compassion, she turned to after her husband's suicide come to appear less the free-standing acts of a nymphomaniac than those of a woman trying to find momentary relief or "protection" without having deeply personal demands placed on her. Blanche sought to "fill [her] empty heart" at the same time that she reaffirmed a sexuality lost on Allan's attraction to men and "denied" the death of so many of her relatives. As Stanley himself says, "They [the 'strangers'] got wised up after two or three dates with her and then they quit, and she goes on to another, the same old line, same old act, same old hooey!" This suggests that these "strangers," in "wising up" to Blanche's thinly disguised cries for help and devotion as well as to the artifice and affectation of her ways, were as much to blame for her panic-driven promiscuity as she herself was.

To be sure, the nobility and grandeur of Blanche's character are marred by her intemperance, be it manifested through her passion for drink, her appetite for sex, or her intolerance of Stanley's life-style (all of which she strives with varying degrees of willpower, and success, to overcome). But it is not this flaw which brings about her downfall. Neither is it her predisposition to gloss over the harsh realities of life by pretending that they are simply not there, as is popularly believed. (This "flaw" is responsible for her very survival as much as it is for her adversity.) In any case, it is not flaws which precipitate the downfall of great tragic characters. "Truly dramatic flaws," notes Bert O. States in *Irony and Drama,* "are such as . . . to make [tragic heroes] ambiguously fallible," are what "rescues [them] from perfection in the process of being doomed." Blanche DuBois may fall short of traditional greatness as tragic heroine, but doomed she is from the first by the "very different circumstances" under which she grew up and against which she struggled long after Stella had fled to New Orleans. The absence of truth and intimacy from life at Belle

Reve is what drove Blanche into an early marriage and on the road to calamity, as is the stagnancy, the decadence, of postbellum plantation life what prompted her sister to opt for the vitality of New Orleans and marriage to a man whose virility could never be questioned. Thus, Blanche's clash with Stanley, specifically, her condemnation of him to Stella at the end of act 1, scene 4, cannot be construed as the sole, absolute cause of her downfall, without whose occurrence, say, her troubles would eventually have vanished or before which they could scarcely be said to have been pressing. On the contrary, such clash must be viewed as the *result* of her attempt to achieve an intimacy with Stella which had never before existed between them. It is an inevitable *addition* to a long line of unfortunate incidents stemming from the failure of communion over many years to pervade the lives of the DuBois men and women.

Blanche does not criticize Stanley the morning after "The Poker Night" simply for the sake of criticizing him, of extolling the virtues of life at Belle Reve at his expense. Her harangue is designed, above all else, to draw her closer to her sister, to unite them in "light" and "progress" against "barbarianism." Blanche wishes to "get out" and "make a new life" at this point, not so much because she fears Stanley will destroy her as because she deplores his way of life, whose corrupting influence, she feels, prevents her from attaining intimacy with Stella. Departing Stanley's company alone will do her no good, and she knows it. Her sprightly attraction to him in act 1, scene 2, in spite of his coarseness, tells us she has probably run into his general type in the past, and we are well aware that her flight from Laurel and the assorted "types" of the Hotel Flamingo, among other spots, has done little to alleviate her distress. Escaping Stanley in the company of Stella will lead, she hopes, to the solidification of a bond between them, to their increased compassion for each other's lot, and, consequently, to a new life some place where the past might at least be brought fully to light, if not somehow atoned for.

Even as Blanche's attack on Stanley at the end of act 1 has as its foremost objective convincing Stella to leave him and join her, *not* pointing out the shortcomings of "unrefined types," so too does Stanley's failure to come forward and challenge his sister-in-law's remarks have as its objective, finally, less the secret plotting of sweet revenge than the testing of his wife's loyalty toward him. The crux of these moments, then, is the establishment of Stella as an object of contention, not of Stanley and Blanche as mortal enemies. This is why I say "Stanley's failure to come forward" rather than "his decision not to." He does not decide instantly to conceal his presence and figure out how to get back at Blanche upon overhearing bits of her tirade. He *fails* to confront her at once, I believe, because he is as much befuddled by her use of language and her line of reasoning as he is angered by the epithets "common," "animal," "sub-human" and "brute." Blanche brings an element of complexity to his life here that he fails to comprehend. Incapable of coming forward to defend his way of life—the only way he really knows—in words against hers, he hesitates, his attention directed, not unreasonably, to Stella's reaction to her sister's observations. That Stella responds with, "Why, yes, I suppose he is," to Blanche's "Well—if you'll forgive me—he's *common!*" and, "Go on and say it all, Blanche" to her, "You're hating me saying this, aren't you?" must not be overlooked as a key to the explanation of Stanley's be-havior at this juncture. Stanley cannot be absolutely certain whether Stella is defending him or agreeing with Blanche against him (Stella sits in the armchair, her back to him, in the acting edition of the play; also, he has just entered the apartment when the first exchange of dialogue transcribed above takes place). Therefore, rather than step forward and force the issue too soon, he waits apprehensively for that moment which will afford him the best cover and his wife the best opportunity to prove without question her faithfulness to him. With an assist from a passing train, the moment arrives. Seconds after Blanche exhorts Stella, "*Don't—don't hang back with the brutes!*" Stanley calls out his wife's name outside a closed front door. Stella answers by throwing herself "fiercely" at him, and, in the acting edi-tion, he obliges by "swinging her up with his body." In a word, she chooses to hang back with her brute.

Often too much is made in production of Stanley's grin over Stella's head at Blanche here. I would interpret it as one of supreme, perhaps even smug, satisfaction at Stella's choice of action, as his signal of victory to Blanche. To make more of it than this, to make it the knowing or vicious grin of a man hot for revenge, is to suggest that Stanley eavesdropped de-liberately and maliciously, intent from the first on one day soon venting his full wrath on this woman so disparaging him. But, as I have attempted to show, Stanley's concern during Blanche's speeches is more with Stella's reaction to their gist and tone than with their every word and notion. The idea of revenge can enter his mind only after he is assured of Stella's con-tinued affection and allegiance, if indeed then. And this "revenge" would take the form of proving Blanche to be as "common" as he is, if not more so, of proving his suspicions about her past to be true. That he would plan rape here, having discovered the clue to its suitability as a mode of revenge in Blanche's "sexy by-play" during act 1, scene 2, as Signi Falk intimates in *Tennessee Williams,* is, in my judgment, nearly inconceivable. It would simply not have served Williams's purposes to portray Stanley completely in the negative light of plotting destroyer here. The point of Stella's union with her husband at the end of act 1, scene 4, is neither to play up Blanche's role as unjustly doomed, harmless underdog to Stanley's sinister destroyer, nor his as wholesome protector against her deservedly damned, depraved homewrecker. It is to accent the intimacy Stanley and Stella enjoy and for which Blanche yearns, but from which she is excluded. The play *as literature* easily resists the temptation to define the world solely in terms of extremes, of good and bad, right and wrong, strong and weak, even if facile commercial productions of it often do not.

To claim, for all that, as Signi Falk, among others, does, that "part of the confusion in [*Streetcar*] arises from Williams's glowingly wistful admiration for Stan and his friends and for their capacity for unlimited physical pleasure," together with "his sentimental support and sympathy for Blanche, who degenerated pitifully with the same kind of physical indulgence," is not to analyze carefully moments like those at the close of scenes 3 and 4 of act 1, but to ignore completely the playwright's reasons for their inclusion. These do not exist apart from the rest of the play, the products solely of Williams's incontinent infatuation with the peculiar blend of "childhood innocence" and "vibrant sexuality" to be found in "elemental people." They are not in virulent contradiction to his obvious sympathy for Blanche as a doomed representative of civilization and refinement, or more accurately, of a specific tradition whose effeteness and essential frigidity she seeks to escape, tragically, through impulsive indulgence in carnal pleasures. Perhaps this notion arose in response to the assertion on the part of such noted critics as Brooks Atkinson and Joseph Wood Krutch that the play was about "an unequal contest between the decadence of a self-conscious civilization and the vitality of animal aimlessness," between "decaying aristocracy" and "vigorous barbarism." It may appear so on the surface, but it is not. As I stated earlier, Blanche's struggle in *Streetcar* is not so much with Stanley as with herself in her efforts to achieve lasting intimacy.

Critics most often point specifically to the end of act 1, scene 3, when they charge that there is confusion in the play regarding the placement of its author's sympathies. But their objections to the reunion of Stanley and Stella after the tumult of the poker night as thematically disruptive and filled with a pathos too universally human fail to take into account, tellingly, the part Blanche plays in the situation. The reservations seem based, curiously, on a consideration of the moment virtually out of context. Williams, it is true, does not give us a scene between the two sisters on the balcony of the Hubbell apartment in which Blanche pleads for Stella not to return to Stanley, but he is wise not to. By not including such an exchange of dialogue between the two women (or between Stella and Eunice, for that matter), he conveys the more powerfully by "faint detraction" the idea that there was really never any doubt in Stella's mind that she would return to her husband that night. (Besides, this confrontation need not be depicted here, because it *does* take place in the next scene. Paradoxically, it is the more charged with excitement and suspense for its occurrence *after* the violence and emotion of the previous night, between an even more frenzied Blanche and a Stella completely tranquil after her night of lovemaking with Stanley.) For her, it was only a question of returning at the right moment. It was *Blanche* who suggested she and Stella leave the apartment after Stanley's violent outburst, Blanche who ushered her sister upstairs to Eunice's, not vice versa. And it is Blanche whom Stella leaves upstairs when she comes down to pacify the bellowing Stanley; Blanche who hears, if she does not witness, the emotional reunion of husband and wife; who then "looks into [the] apartment, hesitantly enters, recoils from what she sees, . . . closing [the] door behind her" (acting edition). What does she see? Certainly no violent acts. Yet she expresses terror for Stella's safety, despite Mitch's reassurances. So long excluded from real intimacy, she can only recoil at the sight of her sister in bed with her husband. So secretly envious of them, she can only vent her dismay at their acceptance of violence into their lives. Williams's sympathies are not confused at this point, his readers' perceptions are. Or perhaps they have allowed their memories of the overwrought, conceptually unresolved staging of these moments from the Broadway production or the Warner Brothers film of the play to supersede temporarily their critical acumen. The point of Stanley's and Stella's tearful reunion at the end of act 1, scene 3, is not, then, to make an inconsistent " 'Lawrencian' plea for primitive, spontaneous passion to return to dominance in [the] audiences' lives," as Leonard Berkman phrases it. It is rather to stress the intimacy these two people share, and which is absent from Blanche's life.

Had Williams ended the scene on so strong a note as the reconciliation of Stanley and Stella, critics would be in part justified in taking him to task for muddying his sympathies. But he is careful not to. He has Blanche come down the spiral staircase right after Stanley carries Stella into the apartment. Then, in her moment of painful exclusion from the true intimacy she wants and needs desperately to experience for herself, he reintroduces Mitch to the plot, and with him a sudden ray of hope. The possibility now exists that Blanche might yet secure the intimacy so necessary for her survival and happiness.

In this minor peripety, Williams creates a delicate balance of "all that is possible" in the case of Blanche DuBois. He displays in his treatment of Blanche at the end of this scene what Robert Heilman calls "completeness of understanding," "insight into human division" (*Tragedy and Melodrama: Versions of Experience*). We see her exposed to her own "full sense of flaw," for instance, when she quickly recoils upon looking into the apartment; when she then proceeds to exhibit intolerance in the face of Stanley's and Stella's loving relationship, going so far as to pretend that her sister is subjecting herself to possible acts of violence by spending the night with her husband. We surmise toward the end of act 2, scene 2, that she must have recoiled upon suddenly entering a room she thought to be empty and finding Allan and friend in bed. We discover that she pretended nothing had happened. In addition, that she could not suppress her intolerance in the face of a homosexual love relationship to which her husband was party. Finally, that Allan visited lethal violence on himself after Blanche's unqualified expression of disgust and contempt at the revelation of his homosexuality.

We see Blanche exposed to her own "full sense of excellence" in the final moments of the scene. Her look at Mitch after he takes out the inscribed silver cigarette case is surely one of deep compassion, linking them in their mutual sorrow—she over a young boy, he a young girl. We can envision the great compassion she expressed and the great sorrow she felt in her struggle to keep Belle Reve afloat and her relatives alive. Her final lines in this scene are at once a veiled plea for help and an ominous expression of self-awareness, as are several other short speeches of hers in the play (witness, for example, the *resigned* expression of self-awareness in, "So do you wonder? How could you possibly wonder!".

"This getting everything into the picture is the ultimate sympathy of the author," says Robert Heilman, "It is his way of 'loving' his characters." And it is by means of irony (referring to the very principle of negation itself), according to Bert O. States, that "[the dramatic poet] seeks out the limits of conceivable proportion and disproportion" in the first place. "He passes through irony, one might say, into dialectic, into arguing *both* sides of the problem fully as opposed to taking one side or another . . . [into] naming nature's limits, finding her out without the complacency or sentimentality of presuming that she can be pinned down and 'dealt with' or, to take the equally sentimental view of the fatalist, that she is bent upon the destruction of our species. . . . What this enables him to achieve in the 'synthesis' of his art is a faint replica of infinitude itself." *(Irony and Drama)*. "Nature's limits" for Blanche are, in terms of fate, total exclusion from intimacy, on the one hand, and complete achievement of it, on the other. In terms of character, they are her inability to suppress her intolerance in crises or situations of great stress, on the debit side, and her overwhelming desire to achieve true and lasting intimacy, making her kind, compassionate and devoted, on the credit. The makings of both extremes of fate are contained in the final pages of act 1, scene 3, but irony has already begun to make its presence felt, and will have arrived once and for all in the next scene.

Stanley Kowalski, convinced, based on the stories he has heard and checked on, that Blanche DuBois is nothing but a scheming floozy who would be little perturbed by her failure to deceive Mitch, attempts to maintain intimacy with his friend by exposing her past to him between acts 2 and 3. Then, after purchasing the bus ticket, he reveals to Stella everything he has learned about Blanche's "recent history" in the belief that she will side with him against her sister. He is unsuccessful in gaining Mitch's friendship, and he is wrong about Stella. Blanche DuBois, unable to conceive of her brother-in-law as a loving and faithful, needing and giving, husband, seeks to achieve intimacy with Stella by selling her on Stanley's commonness and bestiality. She fails. And this the morning after her expression of willingness to enter into an alliance with him, however uneasy, to buy the time necessary to secure an intimate relationship. (She says, "Maybe he's what we need to mix with our blood now that we've lost Belle Reve. We thrashed it [the Belle Reve matter] out. . . . I laughed and flirted and treated it all as a joke.") Needless to say, the alliance did not come off.

Indeed, for all her sensitivity and education, as Leonard Berkman has pointed out, Blanche shows little more understanding of Stanley than he does of her. The question in this play becomes, then, one not of opposing, mutually exclusive ways of life locked in mortal combat, but of different ways of life both come to ruin over the basic issue of truth and intimacy in living. Before Blanche's arrival, Stanley and Stella enjoyed, through compromise, an intimate, happy marriage, and in this could be said to have achieved a degree of civilization, of humanity, unequaled by the DuBoises of Belle Reve. Too, if Stanley is so repulsively barbaric, so completely the representative of the Savage State—and, like it or not, this is the sole image of him that most of us carry around in our minds, Marlon Brando's performance notwithstanding—then what is he doing surrounded by the likes of Stella and Mitch, his wife and his best friend, both of whom are in some ways at least as sensitive as Blanche, if not in as desperate need of kindness? (Not accidentally, Stella and Mitch are the only ones who weep at Blanche's departure.) And why would Williams be so careful as to have it pointed up three times that Stanley served in the "Two-forty-first Engineers," and to have Stanley himself brag about his lucky survival at Salerno against the forces of that arch barbarian, Hitler (as he does often, to judge by Mitch's reaction to his speech)? Surely to convey to us his sense of self-esteem, but for another, less apparent reason, too, I suspect: to inform us of his role as a member of "a society which has lost its shape," to borrow a phrase from Joseph Wood Krutch *("Modernism" in Modern Drama)*, of a "rat-race." Stanley's is an overpopulated, war-torn world where tradition and civilization have come necessarily to mean, to many, less continuity and refinement than freedom and survival. He and the Allies did not "win" at Salerno, they had "come through," they survived.

Likewise, Stanley does not come out the victor in any contest with Blanche; he survives. And if Blanche is a loser in her struggle to achieve true and enduring intimacy with another human being, Stanley is also a loser in his struggle to remain intimate with Stella at the same time he deprives her sister of her chances for happiness with Mitch. Life for him and his wife will never be the same again—Williams provides plenty of evidence for this conclusion in the last scene of the play. He has gone behind Stella's back to expose Blanche's lurid recent past in an attempt to keep the former's confidence and loyalty, ironically, and then compounds his guilt by denying, in a lie greater than any Blanche ever told, the rape. Stanley is, therefore, as much a victim, in his own way, of a society which has lost its shape as Blanche. Blind to her problems and needs and disaffected by the complexity of a way of life alien to his own, he conceives of her as the enemy almost from the start, a threat to the stability, if not the very existence, of his household. And in his eagerness to protect that household and its associations, as in Blanche's to *secure* one, it was inevitable that he would eschew the uncertainty of compromise and confrontation for the safety and reserve of self-reliance. In his attempts to expose Blanche's past so as to preserve his intimate "present" intact, Stanley conceals his actions in the present, even as Blanche, in her attempts to construct a past that will help her achieve an intimate "present," conceals the actions of her past.

Both are doomed in their essential, existential isolation. No longer at one with Nature and in rebellion against Fate, as were the protagonists of

Greek tragedy, they are the inhabitants of a world in which, to recall the title of a recent film by the German director Herzog, it is *Everyman for himself and God against all.* Unlike Greek tragedy, which I would call the tragedy of self, of man, Christian tragedy, as epitomized in *Streetcar,* is the tragedy of life, of men. At once burdened with the notion of original sin and tempted with the idea of salvation in the hereafter, Christian man retreats into his mind, becomes uncertain of his position in the universe, and, feeling himself at the mercy of chance, the helpless victim of chance's whims, resolves to insulate himself as much as possible against the arbitrariness, the "cruelty," of life: essentially, the deeds of other men. In this way ever at odds with his fellow men and never at one with himself, he brings about his own downfall at the same time that the specific and final means of destruction comes from without.

Blanche DuBois, the victim of a life without intimacy at Belle Reve, lies about a past she is correct in believing no one will forgive; Stanley Kowalski, the survivor of a world war of murder and destruction, lies about an act which he is correct in assuming no one will forgive. Neither will tolerate the other, since each believes the other a threat to the achievement or maintaining of intimacy in life. Ironically, it is this very lack of tolerance, of real understanding, that causes each to have his chances for or hold on a truly intimate relationship destroyed by the other, ultimately: Blanche's with Mitch by Stanley, Stanley's with Stella by Blanche, inadvertently. And, appropriately, in a final act—rape—from which all true intimacy has been removed. The feeling aroused in the spectator at this is not, to paraphrase W. H. Auden, that aroused in the spectator of Greek tragedy, the tragedy of necessity or fate, of one man, "What a pity it had to be this way." It is that of the spectator of Christian tragedy, the tragedy of possibility or chance, of two or more men, "What a pity it was this way when it might have been otherwise."

It might have been otherwise, but it was not. The form of this sentence defines *Streetcar's* form, at once suffused with incidentality and inevitability, at once a cross between classic and modern tempers. Ironically, Blanche's doom appears inevitable, yet is essentially pathetic: she will never achieve true and lasting intimacy with another human being; at the same time, her tragedy is made to occur incidentally: Stanley rapes her and she leaves for an asylum with some measure of dignity, never having ceased to accuse him. Blanche herself, representative of "the decadence of a self-conscious civilization," is now lucid, now unstable. Defined by "the vitality of animal aimlessness" of the relationships between Stanley and Stella and the slightly older Steve and Eunice, the play's rhythms are like-

wise now violent and passionate, now calm and reconciled. (Brooks Atkinson's categories apply in part here, if his entering them in an "unequal
contest" does not.)

In this unresolved tension of its form and life, more accurately, in the
embodiment of this tension, this dialectic, in the character of Blanche Du-
Bois, *Streetcar* stands as a unique contribution to the body of world dramatic literature. If classical tragedy's completeness, infiniteness, was its insistence on marking for certain destruction the man in the middle, the man
who was neither flawless nor hopelessly flawed, *Streetcar's* is its depiction
of life's workings as inexplicable, ultimately, in terms of fate or chance exclusively, indeed, as seemingly simultaneously inevitable and incidental.
No small part of this "completeness" is the play's marking for spiritual
death Stella and Mitch, the former in a life tortured by self-recriminations
and lived vicariously through her children, the latter in one haunted un-
ceasingly by the thought of love rejected and happiness lost. Through all
this Williams manages, nevertheless, to leave to the Absurdists to come
the task of sacrificing the essential humanity, the excellence and flaw, of
his characters to the vagaries of a world devoid of all order, meaning, and
purpose.

From "Tarantula Arms" to "Della Robbia Blue": The Tennessee Williams Tragicomic Transit Authority

John M. Roderick

Had William Shakespeare written *A Streetcar Named Desire* it would no doubt head his list of "problem plays." It exhibits a curious resistance to traditional interpretation and utterly defies any insistence upon didactic statement. Reflecting a basic duality or ambiguity which renders comfortable critical statements obsolete, *Streetcar* is often labeled Tennessee Williams's *flawed* masterpiece. An appraisal of the play in the tragicomic terms Williams has set before us, therefore, is long overdue. Williams has not written a flawed tragedy in which our final judgments of hero and heroine are clouded. Rather, through intricate structural control, he has approached brilliant tragicomedy. To commit ourselves solidly to a tragic interpretation would be to do Williams a serious disservice and to deny him that element central to the creative arts—control.

With the tragic implications of so many events in *Streetcar*, one is tempted simply to label the play a tragedy, if an imperfect one. What rises again and again, however, to contradict such a position is a comic spirit that continuously puts the audience off balance. Rather than viewing these comic elements as imperfections in a purely tragic mode, then, or the tragic events as weak melodramatic elements in a comic mode, our appraisal should encompass both modes and allow Williams his tragicomic stance with all of its irreconcilabilities. As Aristotle implies by mimesis,

From *Tennessee Williams: A Tribute,* edited by Jac Tharpe. © 1977 by the University Press of Mississippi.

art mirrors life. And if we give credence to Eric Bentley's decree that "contrariety is at the heart of the universe" *(Life of the Drama)*, we need hardly defend the playwright who illustrates this contrariety in his drama. For the playwright with the tragicomic vision, "the double mask of tragicomedy reveals the polarity of the human condition." It is the tragicomic sense of life that allows the dramatist to laugh with and through his characters and thereby "cope with the overwhelming burden of reality" (David Krause, *Sean O'Casey*).

Williams shows a basic duality at the heart of the tragicomic genre. We begin with the traditional elements of a sacred arena suddenly profaned, but in Blanche DuBois and Stanley Kowalski the complexity of this traditional conflict is compounded. Both are simultaneously attractive and unattractive. Each has elements of both the sacred and the profane. Part of this ambivalence lies in the possibility that the play lends itself to a reading on two levels, one social, the other psychological. Although the levels cannot be isolated in a strict sense, for purposes of discussion one may argue that Blanche, as the last vestige of a dying aristocratic culture, is the heroine on a social level. As heroine she represents all that is sacred within this culture—the love for language, the appreciation of art and music, the "beauty of the mind and richness of the spirit and tenderness of the heart." Stanley, on the other hand, represents the crude destroyer and profaner of this aesthetic sensibility. His violent abuse of Blanche is a destruction of a class as well. In the class struggle neither can brook a coexistence with the other. The negative implication of such a coexistence is seen in Blanche's futile plea to her sister, *"Don't—don't hang back with the brutes!"*

In this same speech Blanche underscores the class struggle and the social tensions which lie behind much of the conflict in the play: "He acts like an animal, has an animal's habits! Eats like one, moves like one, talks like one! . . . Thousands and thousands of years have passed him right by, and there he is—Stanley Kowalski—survivor of the Stone Age! Bearing the raw meat home from the kill in the jungle! . . . Maybe we are a long way from being made in God's image, but Stella—my sister—there has been *some* progress since then! Such things as art—as poetry and music— such kinds of new light have come into the world since then!" It is appropriately ironic that Stanley, in the best "well-made" tradition, is overhearing this entire indictment. As the nature of his adversary's position is revealed, the lines of battle are more sharply defined for Stanley.

On a purely psychological level rather than a social one, however, Stanley emerges as hero. The sexually healthy marriage he shares with Stella stands as the sacred arena defiled by the profane intruder Blanche with her sexual perversity. If Stanley is taken at his word when he confides in Stella, the normalcy of their relationship is convincing: "Stell, it's gonna be all right after she goes and after you've had the baby. . . . God, honey, it's gonna be sweet when we can make noise in the night the way that we used to and get the colored lights going with nobody's sister behind the curtain to hear us. (Their upstairs neighbors are heard in bellowing laughter at something. Stanley chuckles.) Steve an' Eunice." And if we believe that any good subplot is a crucial reflection of the grain of the main plot, then Stanley's allusion to Steve and Eunice also fortifies the position that the Kowalskis share a successful marriage. The relationship of the couple upstairs parallels the marriage of Stanley and Stella in every way—from the violent outbursts to the sensual compensations. Even after the Kowalskis' violent argument, Mitch assures Blanche, "There's nothing to be scared of. They're crazy about each other." Steve and Eunice are likewise able to brook such battles.

In direct contrast to Stanley, on the other hand, Blanche represents the epitome of a psychological malaise. Her sexual perversions with schoolboys are in direct contrast to the normalcy of Stanley's aggressive sexuality in marriage. In the role of psychological profaner, Blanche as much as Stanley is to blame for the rape: "We've had this date with each other from the beginning!", he ominously tells Blanche just before he rapes her. And both he and Blanche recognize the truth in his statement. Earlier Blanche confided to Mitch, "The first time I laid eyes on him I thought to myself, that man is my executioner! That man will destroy me, unless—." Similarly, it is against Blanche as profane intruder into his domain as "a richly feathered male bird among hens," that Stanley violently reacts as his role of supremacy is threatened in his own house. When Stella tells him to help clear the table, "He hurls a plate to the floor," and says, "That's how I'll clear the table! (He seizes her arm) Don't ever talk that way to me! 'Pig—Polack—disgusting—vulgar—greasy!'—them kind of words have been on your tongue and your sister's too much around here! What do you two think you are? A pair of queens? . . . (He hurls a cup and saucer to the floor) My place is cleared! You want me to clear your places?" Psychologically speaking, then, Blanche represents the profanation of Stanley's sacred, if crude, marriage. But we must cope with both the social and the psychological levels simultaneously. Thus the ambiguous duality in our appraisal of Stanley and Blanche is encouraged by Williams, an ambiguity which is not central to the genre of traditional tragedy alone.

If, as Nietzsche claims in *The Birth of Tragedy,* tragedy is begot by the clash between the vital force of Dionysus and the controlling restraint of Apollo, can we make the assumption that somehow the combination of these conflicting forces is to be found in *Streetcar*? It appears that Stanley Kowalski readily lends himself to identification with the vibrant celebration of procreation (as emblematic of the "gaudy seed-bearer") and the frenzied irrational energy of Dionysus. But where do we place Blanche DuBois in this scheme of things? She is hardly the stalwart of control and restraint, order and symmetry we normally associate with Apollo. Hers appears to be a false control, an illusory order whose erupting energy negates her stance. She is a tainted Apollonian or a hypocritical Dionysian who does not allow her welled-up emotions their freedom, except for sordid lapses with young schoolboys and infantrymen.

Stanley, too, on closer analysis, defies stereotyped classification. Where he does represent explosive sexuality and impulsive vitality on the one hand, he nevertheless strives on the other, to retain the status quo of his marriage with himself as cock-of-the-roost. He serves as an Apollonian demagogue in his attempts to discredit Blanche's reputation to preserve his own world. For all of his impulsive behavior, Stanley seeks, above all, to retain order and symmetry within his created existence. He has his "Napoleonic code" to fall back upon. On this level, Blanche is the Dionysian disrupter of order. What such paradoxical and tautological statements reveal are the shortcomings inherent in attempting to neatly classify complex art. That Williams resists a clearly defined means of measuring tragedy may indicate that we are not wholly in the realm of tragedy in *A Streetcar Named Desire*.

Insufficient attention has been given to Williams's careful juxtaposition of the tragic with the comic—a juxtaposition which underscores not only the ambiguity of the tragicomic genre but, indeed, the ambiguity inherent in an empirical view of reality. Although John Gassner *(The Theatre in Our Times)* acknowledges the paradoxical rhythms in *Streetcar,* like so many critics he appears to be insensitive to the comic spirit which counterpoints the tragic in Williams's play: "But *Streetcar,* for all its dramatic momentum and surge, is a divided work. Ambiguities split the emphasis between realistic and decadent drama, between normal causation and accident, between tragedy and melodrama." Indeed, Gassner goes so far as to parenthetically disapprove of the theatergoing public that does appreciate Williams's humor: "(It was noticed after *Streetcar* had been running for some time on Broadway that audiences, no longer a typically New York playgoing public, reacted to the play as though it were rather comic and prurient.)."

Karl S. Guthke *(Modern Tragicomedy)* is also insensitive to the comic side of *Streetcar* and thereby misinterprets the play as a "so-called naturalistic tragedy, which usually ends on a note of despair unrelieved by the silver lining that appears in the metaphysical reconciliation and religious assurance of traditional tragedy." The greater irony here is that Guthke is dealing precisely with this "bastard genre" tragicomedy and overlooks its most common characteristic, irreconcilability, in a play like *Streetcar*. Traditional reconciliation *is* denied by Williams, but in a tragicomic vein, not in an exclusively naturalistic one.

As a significant parallel to the main conflict between Blanche and Stanley, the relationship between Mitch and Blanche serves well to illustrate Williams's contrapuntal technique of juxtaposing the comic with the tragic. Mitch represents the comic contrast to Stanley in almost every way. While Stanley is solidly built, Mitch tends to be on the heavy side, if not somewhat flabby. Stanley is the "gaudy seed-bearer," and Mitch is an anally fixated momma's boy. Similarly, in his first scene with Blanche, Stanley removes his shirt, saying, "Be comfortable is my motto." In contrast Mitch is ashamed of the way he perspires and to his discomfort wears an alpaca jacket in the hottest weather. With these apparent distinctions the audience can more easily laugh at Mitch's ludicrous affectations in his attempts to impress Blanche.

Through Mitch, Williams succeeds in that juxtaposition of the comic with the tragic central to the tragicomic mode. Following immediately upon the tragic implications of a world rapidly closing in upon Blanche and her desperate efforts to seduce Mitch as a potential husband, for example, Mitch brags adolescently that his stomach "is so hard now that a man can punch me in the belly and it don't hurt me. Punch me! Go on! See?" And as Blanche continues to make overtures, Mitch misses the sexual implications altogether and says, "Guess how much I weigh Blanche?" When he hesitates and realizes that his weight is not such an "interesting subject to talk about," for a split second the audience feels that he may turn to more serious issues until he counters with "What's yours?" as if, somehow, Blanche's weight *will* be an interesting subject to talk about. This comic obtuseness is sandwiched between two highly dramatic and potentially tragic confidences which Blanche shares with Mitch—her belief that Stanley will eventually destroy her and her sense of guilt for destroying Allan Grey, as she recounts the incident: " 'Don't go any closer! Come back! You don't want to see!' See? See what? Then I heard voices say— Allan! Allan! The Grey boy! He'd stuck the revolver into his mouth, and fired—so that the back of his head had been—blown away! . . . It was because—on the dance floor—unable to stop myself—I'd suddenly said—'I saw! I know! You disgust me.' "

The conflict between Stanley and Blanche is similarly permeated with humorous incidents counterpointing the dramatic action. When Stanley initially feels slighted at Blanche's intrusion and then learns that she has let the Belle Reve estate slip through her fingers, his adherence to the "Napoleonic code" to justify his claim is quite humorous, as is his list of expert acquaintances who will appraise Blanche's furs and jewelry. Similarly, in the midst of a highly dramatic scene when Stanley relates the details of Blanche's past to Stella and says he has bought her a one-way ticket back to Laurel, Williams inserts the crudely comic, which makes us laugh despite the potentially tragic action.

> BLANCHE: You have such a strange expression on your face!
> STELLA: Oh—(She tries to laugh) I guess I'm a little tired!
> BLANCHE: Why don't you bathe, too, soon as I get out?
> STANLEY (calling from the kitchen): How soon is that going to be?
> BLANCHE: Not so terribly long! Possess your soul in patience!
> STANLEY: It's not my soul, it's my kidneys I'm worried about!

As Wylie Sypher points out, we seek to escape suffering through comedy (*Comedy*). And as Susanne Langer indicates, even in the gallows laugh is the temporary elevation above the terror of the moment (*Feeling and Form*). One may argue that it is this impulse which motivates Williams's inclusion of the comic with the tragic. But Williams's comic reversals are far too systematic and numerous to be relegated solely to the function of release. The comic elements play their role in aggressive self-preservation just as the tragic possibilities invite the antithetical notion of self-destruction. With the defiant juxtaposition of irreconcilables, ambiguity is at the heart of the tragicomic mode.

Ambivalence seems to be the keynote not only to the judgments made on particular characters, but ultimately to thematic statement as well. The two cannot be viewed in isolation, in fact, because one serves as the vehicle for the other. What, in the final analysis, is Tennessee Williams's attitude toward either Blanche DuBois or Stanley Kowalski? For all their obvious flaws, it seems that Williams is also admitting something glamorous in them, some undefinable, appealing trait which ingratiates them to us despite their sordid acts. Williams's sympathies, for example, are certainly with Blanche when her fragile vulnerability carries her to the destructive flame of Stanley's passions. The waste of this aesthete, indeed the destruction of an aesthetic class at the hands of brute power, touched Williams, as it touches his audience.

When Blanche arrives in New Orleans at the beginning of the play, her lines to Eunice serve as a symbolic prophesy of her movement that will echo throughout the play: "They told me to take a street-car named Desire, and then transfer to one called Cemeteries and ride six blocks and get off at—Elysian Fields!" Before she can truly arrive at Elysian Fields—resting place of the blessed dead in Greek mythology—Blanche must travel the sacrificial path from desire to death and be purged for this epiphany. As she tells Stella very early, it is desire that brings her to New Orleans in the first place.

And when Mitch confronts Blanche with the knowledge of the truth about her sordid past, she readily confesses her guilt:

> MITCH: Didn't you stay at a hotel called The Flamingo?
> BLANCHE: Flamingo? No! Tarantula was the name of it! I
> stayed at a hotel called The Tarantula Arms!
> MITCH: Tarantula?
> BLANCHE: Yes, a big spider! That's where I brought my
> victims. . . . After the death of Allan—intimacies with
> strangers was all I seemed able to fill my empty heart
> with. . . . I think it was panic, just panic, that drove me
> from one to another, hunting for some protection—here
> and there, in the most—unlikely places—even, at last, in a
> seventeen-year-old boy but—somebody wrote the
> superintendent about it—"This woman is morally unfit
> for her position!"

It is a guilt, however, for which she is trying to make amends throughout the play. "Now run along, now, quickly!" she tells the Kowalski newsboy. "It would be nice to keep you, but I've got to be good—and keep my hands off children." Indeed, her ritualistic hot baths throughout the play are central to her symbolic purging process. And the suffering or passion necessary for salvation is experienced through her associations with death. The spiritual and physical toll which these deaths have upon her, from the death of Allan Grey for which she feels directly responsible to the deaths of her relatives whose "epic fornications" drained Belle Reve, is readily apparent in her defense to Stella over losing the estate: "I, I, *I* took the blows in my face and my body! All of those deaths! The long parade to the graveyard! . . . You just came home in time for the funerals, Stella. . . . But funerals are quiet, with pretty flowers. And, oh, what gorgeous boxes they pack them away in! Unless you were there at the bed when they cried out, 'Hold me!' you'd never suspect there was the struggle for breath and bleeding. You didn't dream, but I saw! *Saw! Saw!* . . . Death is expensive, Miss Stella!" Later, when speaking to Mitch, Blanche draws the explicit polarity between death and desire:

> Death—I used to sit here and she used to sit over there and death was as close as you are. . . . We didn't dare even admit we had ever heard of it!
> MEXICAN WOMAN: Flores para los muertos, flores—flores . . .
> BLANCHE: The opposite is desire. So do you wonder? How could you possibly wonder!

It is significant that Williams does not wholly condemn Blanche for her indiscretions. Hers, he insists, is too delicate and spiritual a nature to continue to face the harshness of reality. "I don't want realism," she tells Mitch in a frantic plea for sympathy. "I want magic! . . . Yes, yes magic! I try to give that to people. I misrepresent things to them. I don't tell truth, I tell what *ought* to be truth. And if that is sinful, then let me be damned for it!" Where Williams's sympathies lie is quite clear, but he avoids didactic statement, perhaps to a fault to some tastes, when he allows Blanche to be damned, in one sense, precisely for this sin of idealism.

Through her physical and emotional ordeals, however, Blanche has earned a place for herself in the Elysian Fields. She has journeyed from "Tarantula Arms" to visions of "Della Robbia Blue" in Williams's mythic statement. Although soiled by reality, Blanche's passion has by the final curtain earned her the right to wear the robes of the Madonna. Williams's functional use of symbolic language strengthens such a reading as cathedral bells are heard in the background and the callous men at the card table stand for the first time for the entrance of Blanche DuBois. Blanche herself speaks in the exaggerated, archetypal language which suggests epiphany:

> I can smell the sea air. The rest of my time I'm going to spend on the sea. And when I die, I'm going to die on the sea. You know what I shall die of? (She plucks a grape) I shall die of eating an unwashed grape one day out on the ocean. I will die— with my hand in the hand of some nice-looking ship's doctor. . . . "Poor lady," they'll say, "the quinine did her no good. That unwashed grape has transported her soul to heaven." (The cathedral chimes are heard) And I'll be buried at sea sewn up in a clean white sack and dropped overboard—at noon—in the blaze of summer—and into an ocean as blue as (chimes again) my first lover's eyes!

blaze of summer—and into an ocean as blue as (chimes again) my first lover's eyes!

Contrary to much critical opinion, however, Williams is not a didactic writer. He is too complex a playwright to offer a saccharine resolution. Blanche's ritualistic epiphany is, to be sure, a tainted one. The audience is too fully conscious that her destination with this gentle doctor is an insane asylum. Likewise, her vision of salvation is mocked by the intrusive violence between Mitch and Stanley. As tainted as this vision is on the temporal plane, though, it is a positive force on the spiritual level. It is a creation of an ideal illusion in the face of a destructive reality. But Williams also avoids the melodramatic condemnation of the portentous force which helps destroy Blanche. In lieu of this condemnation is the ambivalent admiration of a vibrant life force. Unlike the film version of *Streetcar* which deems it necessary to "punish" the recalcitrant Stanley for his crime against nature, Williams honors him with a partial victory of his own. He has preserved his domain. The threat to his dominance has been carried away by a doctor and a nurse. We are left with a "Marriage—New Orleans Style." The idealization of a Belle Reve union cannot survive the light of day in Stanley's world, as Williams readily admits. Thus, instead of the manipulated, Hayes-dictated Hollywood ending of Elia Kazan, Williams permits Stanley's final gesture. In fondling the breasts of Stella as she holds his child, Stanley points to a future race not of Shavian supermen, but of Stanley Kowalskis.

But perhaps even this victory is tainted. The psychic wounds which Stella must surely feel when she asks Eunice whether she did the right thing in sending Blanche away are real:

> STELLA: I don't know if I did the right thing.
> EUNICE: What else could you do?
> STELLA: I couldn't believe her story and go on living with Stanley.
> EUNICE: Don't ever believe it. Life has got to go on. No matter what happens, you've got to keep on going.

Perhaps it is significant that Stella remains passive to Stanley's overt sexual gesture. Williams's tragicomic vision allows life to go on, but it is a long way from the best of all possible worlds. Tennessee Williams permits reality.

.

Madonna at the Poker Night: Pictorial Elements in Tennessee Williams's *A Streetcar Named Desire*

Henry I. Schvey

Despite the fact that many of his finest works *(The Glass Menagerie, Summer and Smoke)* contain striking visual effects, previous criticism has neglected the importance of pictorial elements in the work of Tennessee Williams. At the conclusion of his *Memoirs* (1975), Williams points directly at the power and concreteness of which the visual artist (as opposed to the literary) is capable:

> The work of a fine painter, committed only to vision, abstract and allusive as he pleases, is better able to create for you his moments of intensely perceptive being . . . van Gogh could capture for you moments of beauty, indescribable as descent into madness.

The above statement is revealing not only with regard to Williams's attitude towards the pictorial arts, but also illuminates a process he actually employs with great success in his own study of a "descent into madness," *A Streetcar Named Desire* (1947).

The present paper will consider three aspects of Williams's use of pictorial elements in *A Streetcar Named Desire:* his reference to a specific painting in the stage directions to the third scene of the play, the play's colour

From *Costerus: From Cooper to Philip Roth: Essays on American Literature*, N. S., volume 26, edited by J. Bakker and D. R. M. Wilkinson. © 1980 by Editions Rodopi, Amsterdam.

symbolism, and the importance of various objects which correspond to signs and symbols frequently found in Renaissance painting.

It is significant that Williams's original title for *Streetcar* was *The Poker Night,* and that the title was based on a reference to a painting by Vincent van Gogh, *All Night Café* (1888), in the third scene of the play:

> There is a picture of Van Gogh's of a billiard parlour at night. The kitchen now suggests that sort of lurid nocturnal brilliance, the raw colors of childhood's spectrum. Over the yellow linoleum of the kitchen hangs an electric bulb with a vivid green glass shade. The parlour players . . . wear colored shirts, solid blues, a purple, and red-and-white check, a light green, and they are men at the peak of their physical manhood, as coarse and direct as the primary colors. There are vivid slices of watermelon on the table, whiskey bottles, and glasses.

It is obvious from Williams's description of The Poker Night scene that he has taken great pains over the precise visual effects down to the smallest details of colour and shape. Not only does Williams derive the setting of this scene from van Gogh's work, he even forces his audience to view it in pictorial terms as a *tableau vivant,* adding the stage direction, "For a moment there is an absorbed silence as a hand is dealt."

The resemblance between Williams's detailed stage directions and van Gogh's painting would hardly be worth mentioning were it not for the fact that in "The Poker Night" scene, Williams is concerned not only with external but with internal equivalence. The work, which has been called van Gogh's "most expressionist painting" is dominated by colour contrasts, "color suggesting some emotion of an ardent temperament." Specifically, the canvas is marked by the contrasts of the bloodred walls and yellow floor with dark green, coffin-shaped billiard table set diagonally in the middle, casting an ominous shadow. The eeriness of the scene is further conveyed by the figure of the landlord in his white coat who faces the viewer from behind the table, and especially by the four luminous lamps suspended from the ceiling, which are surrounded by areas of intensely vibrating yellow light. Perhaps the most interesting comment about this painting was made by van Gogh himself in a letter to his brother Theo:

> I have tried to express the idea that the café is a place where one can ruin oneself, go mad, or commit a crime. So I have tried to express, as it were, the powers of darkness in a low public house, by soft, Louis XV green and malachite, contrasting with

yellow-green and harsh blue-greens, and all this in an atmosphere like a devil's furnace, of pale sulphur. And all with an
appearance of Japanese gaiety, and the good nature of Tartarin.

Van Gogh's comments about this hallucinating work are extremely revealing when applied to *Streetcar*. Williams, too, uses striking colour contrasts
in this scene ("the raw colors of childhood's spectrum") to create an atmosphere teeming with potential violence in the men "at the peak of their
physical manhood" who are as "coarse and direct as the primary colors."

The scene (which significantly begins with the words, "anything wild
this deal?") moves from the atmosphere of potential violence to the real
thing, and climaxes in Stanley Kowalski's hurling a radio out of the window, striking his wife Stella, and being forcibly restrained from doing further damage to her by the other poker players who grapple with him and
finally throw him into a cold shower. The scene concludes with a passionate reconciliation between Stanley and Stella in which he "throws back his
head like a baying hound and bellows his wife's name" before they "come
together with low animal moans."

Williams creates an atmosphere of barbaric, jungle-like violence in
twentieth-century America in which Blanche DuBois (who has come to
stay with her sister as a refuge) is first lost and mystified, then trapped and
destroyed. As she says to Stella of Stanley and the poker night:

> Thousands and thousands of years have passed him right by,
> and there he is—Stanley Kowalski—survivor of the Stone Age!
> Bearing the raw meat home from the kill in the jungle! . . .
> Night falls and other apes gather! There in front of the cave, all
> grunting like him, and swilling and gnawing and hulking! His
> poker night!—you call—this party of apes!

To create the savage and primitive atmosphere, the playwright employs
the harsh primary colours of the jungle where "one can ruin oneself, go
mad, or commit a crime."

But Williams not only uses such detailed colour symbolism in this
scene avowedly based on van Gogh's painting, he uses it throughout the
play as a means of articulating the struggle between the play's two antagonists, Blanche DuBois and Stanley Kowalski; a struggle which ultimately
leads to violent rape and Blanche's mental breakdown.

The central conflict in the play may be seen as dramatized through the
use of colour. Although in scene 2 Blanche coyly indicates to Stanley that
she "likes an artist who paints in strong, bold colors, primary colors," it

is her antagonist who is associated with these colours throughout the play: in the opening moments when he returns home bearing "a blood-stained package from a butcher's"; the "gaudy pajamas" that lie across the threshold of the bathroom in scene 4; his green and scarlet silk bowling shirt, which he wears in scene 5 (and which is worn again at the beginning of the rape scene); and in the brilliantly coloured pajama top he waves as a flag before his assault on Blanche.

Even when not actually wearing these articles of clothing, Stanley's speech reinforces the visual connection between himself and bright harsh colours. His pet name for sexual intercourse, for example, is to "get the colored lights going," and the evening of his rape of Blanche he calls "a red-letter night" for both of us. In his description of Stanley in the stage directions, the playwright himself refers to him as "a richly feathered male bird" and "gaudy seed bearer."

Blanche, as her name suggests, is primarily identified (in contrast to Stanley's loud colours) with white, stressing her essential purity, even innocence in the jungle-like world into which she has come as a stranger seeking refuge. Even the first words spoken to her "What's the matter honey? Are you lost?" suggest Blanche's singularity as she arrives in her "white suit with fluffy bodice, necklace and earrings of pearl, white gloves and hat."

In view of the associations made between Blanche and whiteness, it is interesting to note that in the "Poker Night" scene, Stanley throws "a small white radio" which Blanche is listening to out of the window, thus prefiguring—by means of colour—the play's conclusion, when Blanche herself is thrown out of the house by Stanley.

Of course, in view of Blanche's promiscuity (her visit to her sister in New Orleans has been precipitated by her being run out of Laurel, Mississippi), it is possible to view Blanche's identification with white as an ironic use of colour by the author. Ruby Cohn, for example, has seen Blanche's translation of her own name "White woods. Like an orchard in spring," as a fantasy, suggesting that "the purity of Blanche-white is undermined by the thicket of DuBois-woods. Anglicized, Blanche's name is Du Boys, and under her chaste surface, Blanche lusts for boys."

In addition, soon after her arrival, Blanche changes into a red satin robe which she uses to flirt with Stanley, and which she also wears briefly in the play's final scene.

This apparent inconsistency in Williams's use of colour symbolism is justified by Blanche's own nature, which contains both innocence and promiscuity, the latter a result of the shattered dreams of her youth. As

Stella observes, "When she was young, very young, she had an experience that—killed her illusions." However, the essential division in Blanche's character is ultimately resolved by the playwright in the final scene of the play, and, once again, this resolution is indicated to the audience by means of a symbolic use of colour.

When Blanche comes on stage in the final scene, she is wearing her red satin robe, suggestive both in colour and material of Stanley's forced sexual possession of her in the previous scene. As she prepares to leave the house, however, she changes her clothes, and the colour of her new outfit is specifically remarked upon by the other characters.

> EUNICE: What a pretty blue jacket.
> STELLA: It's lilac colored.
> BLANCHE: You're both mistaken. It's Della Robbia blue. The
>   blue of the robe in the old Madonna pictures.

Although Blanche is clearly suffering from complete nervous collapse at this point in the play, the associations between herself and the blue traditionally associated with the Virgin in Renaissance art is by no means an accident. Rather, it is fully consistent with the direction of Williams's symbolism from early on in the play. In the second scene, for example, Blanche sings the following in the bathroom.

> "From the land of sky-blue water, They brought a captive
>   maid."

This song stresses the connection between Blanche, the colour blue, the forced captivity of an innocent maid, and obviously foreshadows the ending of the play when, dressed in blue, she is literally taken captive by the doctor and nurse, and led out of the house . . . "a captive maid!" This change of costume from red satin to blue, at the end of the play, obliges us to see Blanche as casting off her sensual side in favour of a new innocence, with strong implications of spiritual rebirth.

Although the analogy between Blanche and the Virgin Mary suggested by Williams's colour symbolism seems strange, it is fully in keeping with numerous references found throughout the play which reveal that in his representation of Blanche DuBois as a tragic heroine, Williams was thinking of attributes traditionally identified with the Virgin in Renaissance art.

In scene 10, for example, Blanche wears a rhinestone tiara, a crumpled white satin gown, and a pair of scuffed silver slippers with brilliants set in their heels. Even though Stanley scoffs at Blanche's terrible predicament:

"And with that crazy crown on! What queen do you think you are!", the image of Blanche at her most pitiful may be seen as a variation on the familiar image of Mary as Queen of Heaven, portrayed with a crown bearing the twelve stars of the apocalyptic vision (Rev. 12:9). Stanley's sarcastic reference to Blanche as a "queen" is, in fact, taken seriously by the dramatist.

In the following scene, following her rape by Stanley, Blanche appears in the amber light of the doorway. The stage directions refer to her "tragic radiance" and to the "sculptural lines of her body." Ruby Cohn has objected that this scene "borders on sentimentality . . . aggravated by such pretentious stage directions," but if we realize that Williams is trying to create the visual image of the aureole frequently used in pictorial representations of the Blessed Virgin, consisting "of a field of radiance and splendour which encircles the whole body and appears to emerge from it. In some cases the aureole follows the form of the body and clings closely to it, appearing as a fringe of light," the stage directions become more comprehensible.

Williams not only uses colour and light to suggest an analogy between Blanche and the Virgin Mary, but numerous other indications as well. Her astrological sign,—in contrast to Stanley's Capricorn, the goat— is Virgo, and she is ironically referred to by him as a "lily," a flower suggestive of death (and picked up later in the old Mexican woman's cry, "Flores para los muertos") but also traditionally symbolizing the purity of the Virgin amid the sins of this world.

In addition, in the final scene Blanche holds a "silver-backed mirror" reminiscent of the spotless mirror which is one of the attributes of the Virgin. Williams's explicit stage directions informing the reader that her look is of "sorrowful perplexity as though all human experience shows on her face" reminds one of another devotional representation of Mary, that of the *Mater Dolorosa*. The Cathedral bells which chime during the scene and the fact that, when Stanley orders the doctor and matron to remove Blanche by force, Pablo cries, "Madre de Dios! Cosa mala, muy, muy mala" are further indications of Williams's intentions in this scene.

Perhaps the most persuasive piece of visual evidence indicating the religious symbolism underlying the final scene of *Streetcar* is Williams's manipulation of Stella's child. Unlike Esther Merle Jackson, who states that the playwright "exposes [Blanche's] progress toward the last circle of hell," I would argue that to see the last scene only in terms of Blanche's fall is to miss Williams's true intention which is to suggest not "the ultimate point of descent" but to indicate that Blanche's tragic destruction on one level, may be seen as heroic transcendence on another. It is for this reason that scene 11 is filled with imagery suggesting not merely death, but rebirth as well.

Stella's baby, born at approximately the same time as Blanche's violation by Stanley in the previous scene, is associated with Blanche in the final moment of the play. As Blanche leaves followed by the doctor and the matron, Stella cries out "Blanche! Blanche, Blanche!" Her cry is of course not answered in words, but the visual action suggests a kind of response to her cry; "(Eunice descends to Stella and places the child in her arms. It is wrapped in a pale blue blanket. Stella accepts the child, sobbingly.)" By giving her the child in answer to her plea for Blanche who is leaving, and by having the child wrapped in a *pale blue blanket,* a colour we have come to associate with Blanche, Williams clearly suggests an identification between the tragic fall of one and the birth of the other. In the light of Williams's colour symbolism throughout the play, this exchange may be seen as a suggestion that Blanche's symbolic death has ultimately resulted in new life.

This connection between death and rebirth, so essential to Christian doctrine, is further conveyed by the fact that the baby's birth is celebrated by a bunch of grapes, a traditional symbol for the blood of Christ and the wine of the Holy Communion, and these grapes are immediately associated in the mind of Blanche with her own death:

> You know what I shall die of? (She plucks a grape.) I shall die
> of eating an unwashed grape one day out on the ocean . . .
> "Poor lady," they'll say, "the quinine did her no good. That
> unwashed grape has transported her soul to heaven."

Thus Blanche's fall, prefigured at the very outset of the play when she describes her journey ("They told me to take a streetcar named Desire, and then transfer to one called Cemeteries and ride six blocks and get off at Elysian Fields!") is actually part of a process which goes beyond death and hints at something like heroic transcendence, which is conveyed in the measured tones of Blanche's final words, "Whoever you are—I have always depended on the kindness of strangers," so full of tragic irony for the sister who has consented to her removal.

Through a careful examination of the play's pictorial elements, it has become clear that the end of this play is not so much a "descent into hell" as an expression of spiritual purification through suffering.

The Fate of the Symbolic
in *A Streetcar Named Desire*

Kathleen Hulley

To reconcile literature and theatre is not to compromise and lose something from each, but rather to understand what dramatic dialogue is and does, why words on the page are not the same in function as words on the stage. The methods of literary criticism may well be inappropriate by themselves: we are not judging the text but what the text makes the actors make the audience do.
    J. L. STYAN, *The Dynamics of Drama*

Styan points out what we too often forget in writing about theatre: that theatre does not exist except through the presence of an audience. Martin Esslin tells us of an actress Max Frisch saw walking across a stage. She was simply walking, eating an apple, somewhere, anywhere. However, because for Frisch she was walking across a stage, the moment suddenly blazed with significance. For Frisch the importance element was a stage; for me, it is the presence of Frisch. If he had not been there, as the audience, the event would have had no meaning at all. The sacred powers of the stage are utterly dependent on the presence of an audience, which tacitly agrees that what happens on the stage is *not* life but its magic simulacrum.

Because of this convention, the stage is the semiotic space par excellence. Every artifact, every gesture, every word on the stage is symbolic because nothing on the stage refers to itself; by its very presence on the stage, the simplest chair becomes a symbol of reality, but is not reality. It

---

From *Themes in Drama,* edited by James Redmond. © 1982 by Cambridge University Press.

gestures away from itself and toward a world exactly like ours but else-where. The stage *re*-presents reality; it doubles it, but it is not it.

Theatre is thus nothing but a system of signs, a crossroads through which the symbolic functions. Nothing on stage has meaning except through the presence of an audience. Thus the theatre is the space where we see functioning what O. Mannoni has called "l'autre scène." The concept of *the other scene* is useful because it uses the structure of the theatre to demonstrate the structure of desire in three ways. First of all, what is on the stage points to another scene, just as desire must always be for what is absent. Second, the stage points to that absent scene only because of the presence of the *other*—the play's audience, the desired object—to whom the play, or desire, is directed. Finally, the distinction between the objects on the stage and the objects in the "real" world is possible only because the members of the audience share a discourse, not their own, but that which makes of them an audience so that, like desire, they are created by a culture or ideology outside themselves. This last *other* is the language of codes and conventions into which we are born and which we acquire in learning to speak. It is through this discourse that we define ourselves as "normal," "male," "female," "audience," and so on. Without reference to the *other scene,* neither theatre nor desire exists.

Theatre demonstrates, therefore, that signs do not signify; rather, one sign points to another sign. Neither has meaning except in an ecology of relationships. Because of this ecology, the theatrical artifact functions as a "trace" in the Derridian sense; it marks an absence, it makes possible what has not yet come into existence, it marks the *other scene.*

Derrida says of the "trace":

> The (pure) trace is difference [sic]. It does not depend on any sensible plenitude, audible or visible, phonic or graphic. It is, on the contrary, the condition of such plenitude. Although it *does not exist,* although it is never a *being-present* outside of all plenitude, its possibility is by rights anterior to all that one calls sign.

The sign on stage functions like the trace because its emptiness marks the possibility of desire so that desire may exist.

In *Streetcar,* Blanche's neurotic symptoms do the same work as the trace in language: they have no meaning but they create the condition for meaning. Elia Kazan, the director of the first major production of the play, conceived of the character of Blanche as a series of roles and changing masks which called to the powers of belief in the characters around her.

But *Streetcar* is more than a series of changing masks; it is a series of productions or stagings in which each of the central characters—Blanche, Stella, Stanley—interchanges the positions of actor, director, and audience. This interchange empties any sign or role of meaning and places meaning in the play's audience. Any "reality" to which the stage refers is purely a construction of its audience.

Alvin B. Kernan points out that the "play turns on a fundamental similarity between life and the stage, and the problem of an individual constructing a life and an author constructing a play." If this is so, the play leaves in suspension any solid base for meaning; both the scene and its points of reference (life) are "constructions." Because *Streetcar* makes this analogy between life and theatre specific, it represents, doubles, and thereby deconstructs the process by which meaning is produced.

The process is dramatized through a deconstruction of the forces controlling desire. The first of these Williams treats thematically through the relation between desire and hysteria. The second of these is the symbolic level of Williams's manipulation of our relation to the setting. The third is ideological as he represents the function of the audience's interpretation of desire.

The epigraph of *Streetcar* is from Hart Crane:

> And so it was I entered the broken world,
> To trace the visionary company of love, its voice
> An instant in the wind (I know not whither hurled)
> But not for long to hold each desperate choice.

This citation directs us to Williams's thematic and structural concerns: the brevity and incompleteness of desire. The poem reflects a fractured Platonism—the world we know merely shadows the traces of an ideal love which we grasp only in fragments. More importantly, that broken world is exactly analogous to theatre—a partial space we enter to watch a shadow play which represents some other desired space.

The thematic level—hysteria—gives rise to important issues of the play. Freud has suggested that hysteria produces signs or symptoms which are both signs of the disease and signs of the causes of the disease, but not, in fact, either. Thus, a symptom, like the mask, points both away from and toward itself. According to Mannoni, hysterical symptoms, such as those that Blanche manifests, are a series of roles or masks which hide an absence. In *Clefs pour l'imaginaire,* Mannoni describes the close relation between the masks of hysteria and the masks of theatre:

> The subjects who are termed histrionic represent themselves "dramatically"; they play the roles of love, jealousy, outraged honor as well as mourning or jubilation in order to defend themselves against an insufficiency in experience—against the feeling of their own nothingness.

In theatre, on the contrary, even though the actor plays a number of roles, none of which is his own, the conventions of the stage allow the roles, which mark an absence, to assure us of the presence of *something* elsewhere. The actor playing love is not in love, but he assures us that love exists because it can be indicated. The difference between the absence behind the hysteric's roles and the absence behind the actor's roles lies not in the roles but in the *conventions* which govern the audience of theatre and the audience of hysteria.

It is precisely because of these theatrical conventions that the symbolic register of *Streetcar* begins with the initial setting of the play. We enter the play through a series of specifications which are ambiguously "realistic": the street is named "Elysian Fields," the streetcar named "Desire." The house, "weathered grey with rickety outside stairs and galleries," sits on a most unnatural street. The sky is tinted an artificial shade of "tender blue, almost turquoise," and a blues piano provides unceasing background music, drowning out the more realistic sounds of the river and the railroad (both unseen). Two women, one white one black, guard the entrance, and their opening dialogue overlays a surrealistic montage of disconnected, meaningless fragments—"St Barnabus," "Blue Moon Cocktails," "Red Hots," "Four Deuces," the sound of prostitutes tapping at shutters. This set is meant to indicate reality, but it increasingly functions as a mask.

Indeed, in scene 3, Williams heightens the artificiality, insisting that the set look nothing like reality but like a van Gogh painting—a representation of a representation. This accumulating artificiality subtly disarms the viewer by a gradual shift toward unreality: we must disavow a realistic set just as we must disavow a real face—"that is not me," we say, in relief; we do not feel impelled to disavow a mask. Thus, the set subverts our defenses against whatever it, in fact, does represent, as it allows the emotional and psychic symbols of the play to speak to us directly.

Finally, the artificial aspect of the opening scene has one other function; it creates the community of *otherness* among the members of the audience. The play calls to the audience from other texts—from mythology, from conventional symbolism, from poetic tradition. "Elysian Fields," for example, is no more than a street sign, but because of the community of literary tradition it refers ironically to another text. This reference both unifies the audience and draws it into the construction of the scene.

The theme of hysteria and the set's artificiality are, indeed, both rhetorical devices which indicate "this is just make-believe"; the play's reality lies, as Blanche knows only too well, in the audience. The meaning of the production devolves, therefore, on the ideology of another scene which gives the theatrical sign its power. This ideology also makes of the audience the functioning pivot between the paradoxical unity of the *signified* and its *signifier* on the one hand, and the impossibility of their identity on the other. The problem is that if the audience is the center of meaning, its power is contradictory, for the audience is both utterly subjective and utterly conventional. The subjective aspect of the audience runs the risk of allowing unlimited meaning while the conventional aspect runs the risk of tyrannizing meaning. Blanche's ability to shift masks is Williams's mode for exploring both the dangers and the freedom inherent in the audience's construction of meaning.

In *Jokes and Their Relation to the Unconscious,* Freud states that the pleasure we feel when suddenly released from the necessity to "make sense" or behave within the syntax of convention can verge on ecstasy. The unrestrained production of meaning, which the shifting categories of humor imply, allows a glimpse of perfect freedom—a moment of absolute revolt against the prevailing codes of order, that primal moment when the world is simultaneously unified and unbound.

However, the implications of the freedom Blanche enacts mirror the dangerous aspects of our own role as audience. For the hysteric's assertion that any role simply represents another role, which can signify yet another role in an infinitely opening series of reflections, suggests that the "real" can never be reached, only signified. The origin of signification lies always beyond, absent, yet continually producing signs of its existence.

It is clear that both the symptoms in hysteria and the act of interpretation rest on the assumption that, in Mannoni's terms, "one thing can always represent another." To interpret is to suppose that in the scene there is a meaning which lies beyond the scene. Commentary reveals not what is said but what was *meant* to be said, and echoes the convention that the signifier represents something other than itself. Theatre, hysteria, and commentary spring from the same assumptions about the nature of meaning: that meaning lies beyond what is revealed, and is absent from what is present. These assumptions, once again, place the audience in the dominant position because they fill with significance the emptiness opened by the sign.

In *Streetcar* the shifting categories of meaning are carefully structured through a shifting series of texts and contexts, each of which displaces the other and each of which puts context-making into the forefront. The first *textual* context is Crane's epigraph, which makes of the reading a literary experience. The first *scenic* context is the rickety house framed by its street with its artificial name, the whole framed by the sounds of the street. The walls of the Kowalski house are organized like a stage within a stage—its two rooms the simultaneous scene of different productions, each played against the other. The bathroom suggests, ironically, a behind-the-scenes scene where various roles, lines, entrances and exits are prepared. The house itself is framed by illusory walls which dissolve in the climactic moment; while the stage frames the set, the audience frames the stage, and the world, to which the stage refers, bustles indifferently outside.

Blanche erupts into this claustrophobic setting like a wild atom from another molecular structure—that "Belle Reve" which never was. But she has already been carefully placed in the opening scene. As the two women in scene 1 joke about Stanley and Stella, it is clear not only that Stanley "has taught Stella to catch his meat," as Ruby Cohn so aptly puts it, but also that this relation is communally fixed and ritualized. Blanche is an intruder in a functioning community. It is not her arrival, but the disjunction we are made to perceive between Blanche and the setting that unleashes the chain of action and sets the streetcar named Desire on its wild course.

It is this disjunction which threatens the boundaries of the permissible and puts the seat of power, both within and without the play, in jeopardy. Blanche is literally and symbolically dangerous because she is too multivalent to be contained; she opens too many possibilities.

Clearly she is disruptive because no matter what she is—fake or genuine, whore or puritan, even sane or insane—she multiplies desire. She herself wants too much—too many men, too much money, her irretrievable youth, purity, love, a home. She wants the reversal of time, two things at once, the impossible, the nonlinear, the forbidden. Moreover, she multiplies desire in others: she makes Stella, for the first time, dissatisfied with Stanley; she offers Mitch escape from his sickly mother; she flirts with Stanley. While Williams creates tremendous sympathy for Blanche's longing for "what *ought* to be true," he has Blanche explicitly equate uncontrolled desire with death—the ultimate loss of identity and meaning. Blank and uncontrolled herself, Blanche erases the marks and codes which make human community possible.

From the moment Blanche and Stanley encounter each other, the play becomes a struggle between them for control of these codes. They do not struggle for territory, but to define what territory will signify. They compete with one another to produce a staging which will elicit from Stella and Mitch the desired definition of territory.

Blanche walks into Stanley's set and begins rearranging his scene. Her trunk is full of costumes for her own varied parts, and she assigns roles to everyone else as well. Stella must become the discontented wife; Mitch, Blanche's "Rosenkavalier"; the young boy, her "prince from Arabian Nights." Stanley, Blanche says, is "simple, straightforward, and honest, a little on the primitive side," a "man." For Blanche, this is not an assessment, it is the role she assigns Stanley.

The success of Blanche's staging depends on her audience. If they believe, her play becomes "what *ought* to be"; if they do not, it remains false. We have seen that the audience is an audience only by a set of conventions which are established by the codes of theatre. Therefore, while there are various possible interpretations of the signs emitted on the stage, the audience is bound to interpret those signs only within the codes of the play and the codes of theatre. As a result, the play balances not so much, as Kernan has suggested, on the "difference between truth and falsehood, real and illusion," as it does on the *discourse* about truth or falsehood, real or illusion. Consequently, the play dramatizes that meaning can be shifted when framed by varying social codes and conventions. Thus, the central issue of *Streetcar* is not merely meaning, but the structure of power that gives a sign a context which determines its meaning. Williams explores this structure by dramatizing the issue of contextual control in the theme of sexual control.

There is nothing new in this. Control of social context has always been an issue, in part at any rate, of sexual control. Lévi-Strauss has pointed out that, because the incest prohibition is universal, it is fundamental to any social order. However, what is important about this prohibition is not its context, but its negative function. The incest prohibition is the NO which bars desire from unlimited production; it is the law which makes social exchange, and therefore, communication, possible. According to this theory then, the social contract, which makes meaning possible, is the map of permissible desire.

Stanley makes explicit the interdependence of contextual and sexual control when he tranforms Blanche's "make-believe" about the past into "lies." Furthermore, when he takes over the definition of Blanche's sexuality, he exchanges his role as audience to her play for the role of producer of his own. This interchange itself is a semantic act which limits the field meaning where desire can function. Stanley maps out Blanche's area and determines her future.

However, Stanley's definition is more than simply one other possible meaning. Stanley lays down the *law* which makes meaning possible. Without law to mark the *differance,* the ecology of the sign collapses. Thus, when Blanche provokes Stanley's resistance, she invites the block which makes the symbolic function. Neither she, nor her symptom/symbols can continue to produce without limit; the end of such production is the end of meaning.

Nevertheless, though Williams has Stanley impose the law necessary to meaning, Williams does not necessarily support the meaning Stanley imposes. Indeed, as Stanley and Blanche wrestle for control of the context, they dramatize several possible strategies for dealing with the symbolic. Blanche's desire may be subversive, but she invites an imaginative interpretation which will form her flood of signs into some vision of the good and the beautiful. The illusions she creates call to the transformative powers of her audience. Indeed, she invites Mitch to share with her the creative moment which would have made love possible. Stanley's law, on the contrary, blocks creativity and puts an end to love. His vision is both antidialectic and antimetaphoric. He restricts the powers of the symbolic function to their most socially expedient level.

Neither Blanche nor Stanley, therefore, is able to play in the interface between desire and the law. Each is excessive in need; neither grows toward a lucid relation to the construction of reality. Consequently, neither paradox nor contradiction has energy in Williams's world. Instead, in *Streetcar* Williams presents a fundamentally enraged vision of a sterile world where meaning has become merely a function of social use.

The power Stanley draws upon to fix meaning resides in three locations: in the characters, in the setting, and in the audience. These three loci determine the control of desire along socially useful lines and allow Williams to expose what he sees as the mechanisms of repression in the dominant system of meaning.

First of all, the characters who surround Blanche and Stanley—Stella, Mitch, Steve, Eunice, the poker players—function as the chorus. They witness events and elevate the quarrel between Blanche and Stanley to the level of ritual by making it significant to the surrounding community. But the choral function depends on stability. It is impossible for the chorus to make events significant without a fixed point from which to view the shifting possibilities. Its ceaseless demand for limits implies that when desire exceeds bounds, both the community and the function of the chorus disintegrate. Chorus and community are each founded on a principle of prohibition.

The chorus must construct the social myth of "reality" and exclude any threat to that myth. In this function, the chorus dramatizes the conventional basis which creates the play's audience. Furthermore, the chorus deconstructs the hermeneutic function of convention; the chorus both extends meaning beyond the personal and limits that meaning.

When the chorus in *Streetcar* allows Stanley to exclude Blanche, it allows the exclusion of that which makes love and art possible. Instead, it limits the possible interpretations of Blanche's roles to their most fundamental level and destroys any rapprochement between the demands of art and the demands of community.

However, if Blanche and Stanley fail to resolve this issue, Williams does not. His setting functions in opposition to his theme by subverting the opening "order" of the setting. The play begins with clear distinctions between inside and out, home and street, marriage and prostitution, black and white. But by scene 3, Williams has already shifted the context of his set so that it no longer represents reality, but art. By the end of scene 5, the set has moved entirely inward to represent Blanche's subjectivity. The set continues to fluctuate between representing "reality" and "unreality" until scene 10 when the walls dissolve and hellish flames shadow the room while the *Varsouvia* of Blanche's memories dominate any exterior sound; all pretense of order disappears. Instead, nothing holds together and nothing holds apart.

The disintegration at the level of setting is thematically mirrored in Stanley's transgression. When he rapes his wife's sister, he too exceeds the limits of his world. At this climactic moment, every category is threatened; desire transcends bounds. Music, light, space collude in a cacophony of disorder.

As the walls dissolve in scene 10, the chorus loses its place; there is no longer an outside or an inside in which to locate, and the choral function shifts to the audience, which is, by convention, "outside." This is the crucial moment for the audience, the moment in which either it allows the disintegration to continue or it restores order. This is the moment when each member of the audience decides either that Blanche has gotten what she asked for, or that Stanley's insensitive dominance exceeds any sympathy. No matter which attitude we adopt, however, to choose is to carve space up once again into socially accepted territories. Any judgment grants power to Stanley; even to hate him is to impose limits on the unbearable violation.

Stella, in the last scene, occupies a position analogous to the audience; she deconstructs the relation between the subjective and conventional limits of the symbol. Like the audience she has been watching a play performed for another—Blanche's "play for" Mitch. Like the audience, she knows more about Blanche's play than does Blanche's intended audience. In this position Stella can form the point of view which will allow Blanche's "play" to continue, or which will terminate it.

When Blanche's play begins, Stella supports any production so long as she, Stella, feels secure. Judgments about truth or falsehood do not concern her at all. Her problem arises only when it becomes evident that Stanley is staging a different production for the same audience, and that she must choose. She cannot allow both meanings to go on simultaneously without putting her own *mise en scène* in jeopardy.

Stella is forced to take a position and thus frame a context for the conflict between desire and community which have been polarized by Blanche's and Stanley's relation to the symbolic. Unfortunately, Stella must destroy either her marriage or her sister. Furthermore, to choose to believe Blanche is to choose desire but destroy the scene of its expression. To believe Stanley is to secure that scene but empty it of desire. Either choice is cruel; but the disorder created by Blanche and Stanley destroys Stella's privileged neutrality and demands action.

When she restores order by choosing, Stella unmasks the simultaneously repressive and creative function of our own interpretative position. Repression is dramatized by the isolation and expulsion of Blanche's boundless desire; creation lies in Stella's very choice. Though her security has been bought at the price of desire, the moment she chooses Stella begins staging her own drama—"The Happy Marriage of Stanley and Stella Kowalski."

Because her choice is responsible for the play's outcome, the play's ironic conclusion belongs not to Stanley but to Stella. "I couldn't believe her story and go on living with Stanley," Stella cries. She is not deluded by Stanley; rather, her decision is the deliberate preservation of social order. No longer innocent or passive, she too adopts a mask, which by its very presence points ironically to the absence of what it represents.

The capacity of theatre to shift categories and contextual frames, which Brecht, for example, so consciously manipulated, is the same capacity more conventional playwrights have used, at least tacitly, to multiply meanings. The conventions of the stage by which a sign both is and is not what it represents depend entirely on the audience which allows the sign to point in two directions at the same time.

No message, of course, carries meaning without a receiver who shares approximately the same code and context as the sender. The strength of the theatre as opposed to any other message system is that the audience which renders the semiotic system on stage significant has no existence as "audience" except by a prior ideology which renders a "real" person on stage an "unreal" character. Thus, the theatre functions within the same code that defines "reality" and whatever lies beyond it, enabling us to examine the conventions of "reality" in a way no other message system can.

Williams deconstructs this function of the theatre by beginning with a set that signifies "reality" and which poses little threat to the audience: the stage is "there" and "unreal," the audience is "here" and "real." The lifelike aspects of his set allow the members of the audience to remain unaware of the dramatization of their own role; they remain outside events, "objective." Taken strictly at the realistic level, *Streetcar* is about the triumph of Stanley's and Stella's desire.

But Williams undercuts the set's duplicitous surface and subverts the illusion of safety, first by transforming the set into an artificial, unreal space which functions like a mask to disarm the audience; second, by handing the choral function over to the audience; and finally, by using Stella to reveal that no audience is in fact "safe." We are all implicated in the play's meaning, whatever that may be.

Because *Streetcar* is a play about conflicting theatrical productions by the various characters, the action on the stage mirrors the action of the audience watching the play. By doubling that action, the play *re*-presents the audience/stage relationship and brings into evidence the conventions by which the audience creates the distinction between "life" and "theatre." At this level, *Streetcar* is not about the wild triumph of desire, but about desire's destruction. Desire is simply another form of theatre, dependent on social convention for its existence, and, therefore, in bondage to its social function.

Desire is, indeed, replete at the end of the play. Stella is pregnant; family and community will continue. But as Stanley fumbles at Stella's blouse, he has lost his virile stature and seems like a child at his mother's breast; Stella's luxurious weeping is not a lapsing back to the darkness of desire, but grief at her irrevocable loss. The streetcar which brought Blanche to the Kowalski household is not named "Desire," it is named "Cemeteries," and its destination is the land of the dead.

Streetcar draws analogies between the social control of desire and the conventional functioning of theatre in order to represent the death of desire. The problem Williams presents is that to limit the productive power of the symbol is repressive, while to allow the symbol unlimited power is chaos. By representing the either/or categories of contextual control through the death of desire, Williams surpasses the issues of "sane" or "insane," "truth" or "illusion" to expose the ambivalent social law which makes those terms significant.

Chronology

1911	Born Thomas Lanier Williams in Columbus, Mississippi.
1911–18	Lives with mother and sister Rose and maternal grandparents, as father is often away on business. They move often, finally settling in St. Louis, Missouri.
1927	Wins prize for essay, "Can a Good Wife Be a Good Sport?" then published in *Smart Set* magazine.
1928	Visits Europe with grandfather. First story published in *Weird Tales:* "The Vengeance of Nitocris."
1929	Enters University of Missouri. Wins honorable mention for first play, *Beauty Is the World.*
1931	Father withdraws him for flunking ROTC at university. Works at father's shoe company.
1935	Released from job after illness and recuperates at grandparents' house in Memphis, where his play *Cairo! Shanghai! Bombay!* is produced.
1936–37	Enters and is later dropped from Washington University, St. Louis. Enters University of Iowa. First full-length plays produced: *The Fugitive Kind* and *Candles to the Sun.* Prefrontal lobotomy performed on sister Rose.
1938	Graduates from University of Iowa.
1939	First uses name "Tennessee" on "The Field of Blue Children," published in *Story* magazine. Travels from New Orleans to California to Mexico to New Mexico to St. Louis. Awarded $1,000 Rockefeller grant. Begins new full-length play, *Battle of Angels.*
1940	Moves to New York to enroll in advanced playwrighting seminar taught by John Gassner at The New School.
1941–43	Takes various jobs in Provincetown, New York, Macon

(Georgia), Jacksonville (Florida), and St. Louis. Begins *The Gentleman Caller* (later *The Glass Menagerie.*) Works at MGM as scriptwriter.

1944   Awarded $1,000 by the National Institute of Arts and Letters for *Battle of Angels. The Glass Menagerie* opens in Chicago on December 26.

1945   *The Glass Menagerie* opens in New York, wins New York Critics' Circle Award.

1946   *27 Wagons Full of Cotton and Other Plays* published.

1947   *A Streetcar Named Desire* opens in New York. *Summer and Smoke* opens in Dallas, Texas. Wins second New York Critics' Circle Award and Pulitzer Prize.

1948   *Summer and Smoke* opens in New York. *American Blues: Five Short Plays* published. *One Arm and Other Stories* published.

1950   *The Roman Spring of Mrs. Stone,* a novel, published. *The Rose Tattoo* opens in Chicago.

1951   *The Rose Tattoo* opens in New York, wins the Antoinette Perry (Tony) Award for best play. Film version of *A Streetcar Named Desire,* screenplay by Williams and Oscar Saul, released.

1953   *Camino Real* opens in New York.

1954   *Hard Candy: A Book of Stories* published.

1955   *Cat on a Hot Tin Roof* opens in New York. Wins third New York Critics' Circle Award and second Pulitzer Prize.

1956   *Baby Doll,* a film. *In the Winter of Cities,* poems, published. Father dies. Begins psychoanalysis.

1957   *Orpheus Descending* opens in New York.

1958   *Garden District (Something Unspoken* and *Suddenly Last Summer)* opens Off-Broadway. Film version of *Cat on a Hot Tin Roof* released.

1959   *Sweet Bird of Youth* opens in New York.

1960   *Period of Adjustment* opens in New York.

1961   *Night of the Iguana* opens in New York.

1962   Film version of *Sweet Bird of Youth* released. A one-act version of *The Milk Train Doesn't Stop Here Anymore* presented in Spoleto, Italy, at the Festival of Two Worlds.

1963   Full-length version of *Milk Train* opens in New York. Period of depression begins after death of his lover Frank Merlo.

1964   Film version of *The Night of the Iguana* released.

1966   *Slapstick Tragedy (The Mutilated* and *The Gnädiges Fraulein)* opens in New York.

1967   *The Two Character Play* opens in London. *The Knightly Quest: A Novella and Four Short Stories* published.

1968   *Kingdom of Earth (The Seven Descents of Myrtle)* opens in New York.

1969   *In the Bar of a Tokyo Hotel* opens Off-Broadway. Converts to Roman Catholicism. Stays three months in hospital in St. Louis after nervous collapse.

1970   *Dragon County: A Book of Plays* published.

1971   Revised version of *Two Character Play* called *Out Cry* opens in Chicago.

1972   *Small Craft Warnings* opens Off-Off-Broadway.

1973   *Out Cry* (a third revision of *Two Character Play)* opens in New York.

1974   *Eight Mortal Ladies Possessed: A Book of Stories* published.

1975   Receives the National Arts Club gold medal for literature. *Moise and the World of Reason,* a novel, is published. *The Red Devil Battery Sign* opens in Boston. Fourth version of *Two Character Play* opens Off-Off-Broadway. *Memoirs* published.

1976   Revised *Red Devil* opens in Vienna.

1977   *Vieux Carré* opens in New York.

1978   *Creve Coeur* opens in Charleston, South Carolina. *Where I Live: Selected Essays* published.

1979   *A Lovely Day for Creve Coeur,* revised version of *Creve Coeur,* opens in New York.

1980   *Clothes for a Summer Hotel* opens in Washington, D.C. Mother dies.

1981   *A House not Meant to Stand* opens in Chicago. *Something Cloudy Something Clear* opens in New York.

1982   Receives honorary degree from Harvard University.

1983   Dies in February.

Contributors

HAROLD BLOOM, Sterling Professor of Humanities at Yale University, is the author of *Anxiety of Influence, Poetry and Repression* and many other volumes of literary criticism. His forthcoming study, *Freud: Transference and Authority*, attempts a full-scale reading of all of Freud's major writings. A MacArthur Prize Fellow, he is general editor of five series of literary criticism published by Chelsea House. During 1987–88, he was appointed Charles Eliot Norton Professor of Poetry at Harvard University.

ROBERT BRUSTEIN is Professor of English at Harvard University and Artistic Director of the American Repertory Theatre Company. He has published many works on theatre including *The Third Revolution, The Culture Watch: Essays on Theatre and Society*, and *Making Scenes*.

ALVIN B. KERNAN is A. W. Mellon Professor of Humanities at Princeton University. His books include critical studies of Shakespeare and of the genre of literary satire.

JOSEPH N. RIDDEL is Professor of English at the University of California at Los Angeles and the author of *The Clairvoyant Eye: The Poetry and Poetics of Wallace Stevens* and *The Inverted Bell: Modernism and the Counterpoetics of William Carlos Williams*.

LEONARD BERKMAN teaches theater at Smith College. He is author of the play *Really, Now* and many articles on contemporary theater.

C. W. E. BIGSBY is Reader in American Literature in the School of English and American Studies at the University of East Anglia in Norwich. His books include *Dada and Surrealism, Confrontation and Commitment: A Study of Contemporary American Drama, 1959–1966*, and *The Second Black Renaissance: Essays in Black Literature* as well as studies of Tom Stoppard, Joe Orton, and Edward Albee.

127

MARY ANN CORRIGAN teaches drama at the University of California at San Diego.

LEONARD QUIRINO is Professor of English at Western Connecticut State College, Danbury.

BERT CARDULLO is studying dramaturgy at the Yale School of Drama. He has written on Shakespeare and has published numerous articles of film criticism.

JOHN M. RODERICK teaches English at the University of Hartford.

HENRY I. SCHVEY teaches English at Leiden University in the Netherlands. He has written on Dylan Thomas, Sylvia Plath, Lanford Wilson, and Tennessee Williams.

KATHLEEN HULLEY teaches English at the University of North Dakota.

Bibliography

Asibong, Emmanuel B. *Tennessee Williams: The Tragic Tension*. Elms Court, Great Britain: Arthur H. Stockwell Ltd., 1978.

Berlin, Normand. "Complementarity in *A Streetcar Named Desire*." In *Tennessee Williams: A Tribute,* edited by Jac L. Tharpe. Jackson: University Press of Mississippi, 1977.

Bigsby, C. W. E. *A Critical Introduction to Twentieth-Century American Drama 2: Tennessee Williams, Arthur Miller, Edward Albee*. Cambridge: Cambridge University Press, 1984.

Broussard, Louis. *American Drama: Contemporary Allegory from Eugene O'Neill to Tennessee Williams*. Norman: University of Oklahoma Press, 1962.

Brown, John Mason. *Dramatis Personae: A Retrospective Show*. New York: Viking, 1963.

Clurman, Harold. "Review of *A Streetcar Named Desire*." In *Lies Like Truth,* 72–80. New York: Macmillan, 1958.

Cohn, Ruby. "The Garrulous Grotesques of Tennessee Williams." In *Dialogue in American Drama*. Bloomington: Indiana University Press, 1971.

Corrigan, Mary Ann. "Memory, Dream and Myth in the Plays of Tennessee Williams." *Renascence* 28 (Spring 1976): 155–67.

Donahue, Francis. *The Dramatic World of Tennessee Williams*. New York: Frederick Ungar, 1964.

Falk, Signi. *Tennessee Williams*. New Haven: College and University Press, 1961.

Fedder, Norman J. *The Influence of D. H. Lawrence on Tennessee Williams*. The Hague: Mouton, 1966.

Ganz, Arthur. "The Desperate Morality of the Plays of Tennessee Williams." *American Scholar* 31 (Spring 1962): 278–94.

Gassner, John. "*A Streetcar Named Desire*: A Study in Ambiguity." In *Modern Drama,* edited by Travis Bogard and William I. Oliver, 1965.

———. *The Theatre in Our Times*. New York: Crown, 1954.

Gilman, Richard. *Common and Uncommon Masks: Writers on Theatre 1962–1970*. New York: Random House, 1971.

Harwood, Britten, J. "Tragedy as Habit: *A Streetcar Named Desire*." In *Tennessee Williams: A Tribute,* edited by Jac L. Tharpe. Jackson: University Press of Mississippi, 1977.

Hughes, Catharine R. *Tennessee Williams: A Biography.* Englewood Cliffs, N.J.: Prentice-Hall, 1978.

Hurley, Paul J. "Tennessee Williams: The Playwright as Social Critic." *The Theatre Annual* 21 (1964): 40–56.

Jackson, Esther Merle. *The Broken World of Tennessee Williams.* Madison: University of Wisconsin Press, 1965.

Jones, Robert Emmet. "Tennessee Williams' Early Heroines." *Modern Drama* 2 (December 1959): 211–19.

Kazan, Elia. "Notebook for *A Streetcar Named Desire.*" In *Directors on Directing,* edited by Toby Cole and Helen Krich Chinoy. New York: Bobbs-Merrill, 1963.

Krutch, Joseph Wood. *Modernism in Modern Drama.* Ithaca: Cornell University Press, 1953.

Law, Richard A. *"A Streetcar Named Desire* as Melodrama." *English Record* 14 (1966): 2–8.

Leavitt, Richard, ed. *The World of Tennessee Williams.* New York: G. P. Putnam's Sons, 1978.

Londre, Felicia Hardison. *Tennessee Williams.* New York: Frederick Ungar, 1979.

Maxwell, Gilbert. *Tennessee Williams and Friends.* Cleveland: World, 1965.

McCarthy, Mary. "A Streetcar Called Success." In *Sights and Spectacles 1937–1956,* 131–5. New York: Farrar, Straus & Cudahy, 1956.

———. "Oh, Sweet Mystery of Life." *Partisan Review* 15 (1948): 357–60.

Miller, Jordan Y., ed. *Twentieth Century Interpretations of* A Streetcar Named Desire: *A Collection of Critical Essays.* Englewood Cliffs, N.J.: Prentice–Hall, 1971.

Nelson, Benjamin. *Tennessee Williams: The Man and His Work.* New York: Oblensky, 1961.

Popkin, Henry. "The Plays of Tennessee Williams." *Tulane Drama Review* (1960).

Porter, Thomas E. "The Passing of the Old South: *A Streetcar Named Desire.*" In *Myth and Modern American Drama,* 153–76. Detroit: Wayne State University Press, 1969.

Starrow, Constantine N. "Blanche DuBois and Emma Bovary." *Four Quarters* 7 (1958): 10–13.

Taylor, Henry. "The Dilemma of Tennessee Williams." *Masses and Mainstream* 1 (April 1948): 54.

Tharpe, Jac L., ed. *Tennessee Williams: A Tribute.* Jackson: University Press of Mississippi, 1977.

Tischler, Nancy. M. *Tennessee Williams: Rebellious Puritan.* New York: Citadel Press, 1965.

Tynan, Kenneth. "American Blues: The Plays of Arthur Miller and Tennessee Williams." *Encounter* 2 (1954): 13–19.

Vidal, Gore. "Love, Love, Love." *Partisan Review* 26 (1959): 613–20.

Weales, Gerard. *Tennessee Williams.* Rev. ed. University of Minnesota Pamphlets on American Writers. Minneapolis: University of Minnesota Press, 1974.

Williams, Tennessee. *Memoirs.* Garden City, New York: Doubleday, 1975.

———. "On a Streetcar Named Success." In *Where I Live: Selected Essays.* New York: New Directions, 1978.

Acknowledgments

"America's New Culture Hero: Feelings Without Words" by Robert Brustein from *Commentary* 25, no. 2 (February 1958), © 1958 by Robert Brustein. Reprinted by permission of the author and of *Commentary*. All rights reserved.

"Truth and Dramatic Mode in *A Streetcar Named Desire* (originally entitled "Truth and Dramatic Mode in the Modern Theater: Chekhov, Pirandello, and Williams") by Alvin B. Kernan from *Modern Drama* 1, no. 2 (September 1958, © 1958 by the University of Toronto, Graduate Centre for the Study of Drama. Reprinted by permission.

"*A Streetcar Named Desire*—Nietzsche Descending" by Joseph N. Riddel from *Modern Drama* 5, no. 4 (February 1963), © 1963 by the University of Toronto, Graduate Centre for the Study of Drama. Reprinted by permission.

"The Tragic Downfall of Blanche DuBois" by Leonard Berkman from *Modern Drama* 10, no. 3 (December 1967), © 1967 by A. C. Edwards. Reprinted by permission.

"Tennessee Williams: Streetcar to Glory" by C. W. E. Bigsby from *The Forties: Fiction, Poetry, Drama,* edited by Warren French, © 1969 by Warren French. Reprinted by permission of Everett/Edwards, Inc.

"Realism and Theatricalism in *A Streetcar Named Desire*" by Mary Ann Corrigan from *Modern Drama* 19. no. 4 (December 1976), © 1976 by the University of Toronto, Graduate Centre for the Study of Drama. Reprinted by permission.

"The Cards Indicate a Voyage on *A Streetcar Named Desire*" by Leonard Quirino from *Tennessee Williams: A Tribute,* edited by Jac Tharpe, © 1977 by the University Press of Mississippi. Reprinted by permission.

"Drama of Intimacy and Tragedy of Incomprehension: *A Streetcar Named Desire* Reconsidered" by Bert Cardullo from *Tennessee Williams: A Tribute,* edited by Jac Tharpe, © 1977 by the University Press of Mississippi. Reprinted by permission.

131

"From 'Tarantula Arms' to 'Della Robbia Blue': The Tennessee Williams Tragicomic Transit Authority" by John M. Roderick from *Tennessee Williams: A Tribute,* edited by Jac Tharpe, © 1977 by the University Press of Mississippi. Reprinted by permission.

"Madonna at the Poker Night: Pictorial Elements in Tennessee Williams' *A Streetcar Named Desire*" by Henry I. Schvey from *Costerus: From Cooper to Philip Roth: Essays on American Literature,* N. S. volume 26, edited by J. Bakker and D. R. M. Wilkinson, © 1980 by Editions Rodopi. Reprinted by permission.

"The Fate of the Symbolic in *A Streetcar Named Desire*" by Kathleen Hulley from *Themes in Drama,* edited by James Redmond, © 1982 by Cambridge University Press. Reprinted by permission of Cambridge University Press.

Index

Actors Studio, 8–9, 10, 12
Adler, Luther, 8, 10
Aeneid (Virgil), 65
After the Fall (Miller), 47
"Against Interpretation" (Sontag), 77
Allan. *See* Grey, Allan (in *Streetcar Named Desire*)
All My Sons (Miller), 42
Aristotle, 93–94
Atkinson, Brooks, 86, 92
Auden, W. H., 91

Battle of Angels, 41, 49
Bentley, Eric, 94
Berkman, Leonard, 81, 82–83, 87, 89
Birth of Tragedy, The (Nietzsche), 23, 95–96
Blanche. *See* DuBois, Blanche (in *Streetcar Named Desire*)
Brando, Marlon, 13, 15; Stanley Kowalski as portrayed by, 8, 9, 10, 58, 89
Brecht, Bertolt, 120
"Broken Tower, The" (Crane): as epigraph to *Streetcar Named Desire*, 3, 6, 24, 47, 63–64, 113, 116
Brown, John Mason, 34, 39
Buck, Pearl, 41
Burke, Kenneth, 22

Camino Real, 3, 44
Candida (Shaw), 13
Careless Years (Lewis, screenplay and story), 14
Cat on a Hot Tin Roof, 3, 37, 42
Cervantes, Miguel de, 42

Chekhov, Anton, 2, 12, 17, 53
Clefs pour l'imaginaire (Mannoni), 113–14, 115
Clurman, Harold, 56, 58, 79
Cohn, Ruby, 106, 108, 116
Comedy (Sypher), 98
Compulsion (Murphy, screenplay), 11
Conrad, Joseph, 46
Crane, Hart, 2–3, 4, 5, 24

Darwin, Charles, 70–71, 75, 77
Dean, James, 13, 15, 16
Death of a Salesman (Miller), 42
Derrida, Jacques, 112
Directions in Modern Theatre and Drama (Gassner), 60
Divine Pastime, The (Clurman), 56
Doctor, 29, 75
Dramatis Personae (Brown), 34
DuBois, Blanche (in *Streetcar Named Desire*): alcoholism of, 26, 52, 53, 57, 83; and Allan Grey, 81–82, 83, 88, 97–98; ambiguity of, 57, 112, 115; bathing obsession of, 26, 28, 52–53, 59, 65, 69, 72, 99; breakdown of, 3–4, 26, 54, 60, 79, 95, 112; clothing of, 50–51, 54–55; dishonesty of, 36–37, 38, 57, 81, 91; guilt of, 5, 25, 26, 28, 37, 38, 53, 69, 97, 99; and Harold Mitchell, 28, 37–38, 39, 40, 45, 66–67, 83, 88, 90, 91, 97, 116, 118; as heroine, 35, 79, 82–83, 94; illusions of, 17, 18–19, 25, 34, 46–47, 53, 54–55, 56, 57, 59; intimacy's importance to, 35, 36, 37, 38, 39, 40, 52, 57, 66, 83, 86, 87–88, 89, 90–91;

DuBois, Blanche (*continued*)
as intruder, 94, 116; as Madonna, 100, 106, 107–8; as moth, 63, 67, 68, 69, 72, 75, 79; promiscuity of, 4, 38, 45, 83, 94–95; schizoid personality of, 25, 27, 34, 39, 56, 57, 92, 106–7; sensitivity of, 24, 29, 37, 56, 69, 79, 86, 94; sexuality of, 38, 56, 57, 83, 85; spiritual rebirth of, 70, 100, 101, 107; and Stanley Kowalski, 17–18, 25, 26, 35, 45, 47, 50–51, 54, 56–58, 59–60, 69–70, 79, 81, 83, 84–86, 89, 90–91, 94, 95, 116; and Stella Kowalski, 27–28, 37, 82, 84, 85, 87, 88, 89, 90, 116; as victim, 30, 70, 81, 90, 91
Dynamics of Drama, The (Styan), 111

East of Eden (Osborn, screenplay), 14, 15
Edge of the City (Aurthur, screenplay and story), 14
Eliot, T. S., 22, 38
Emerson, Ralph Waldo, 4
Eunice. *See* Hubbell, Eunice and Steve (in *Streetcar Named Desire*)

Falk, Signi, 79, 85, 86
Fall of Hyperion (Keats), 3
Feeling and Form (Langer), 98
"For the Marriage of Faustus and Helen" (Crane), 24
Freud, Sigmund, 2, 24–25, 113, 115

Garfield, John, 8, 10
Gassner, John, 60, 79, 96
Ghost Sonata, The (Strindberg), 69
Giant (Guiol and Moffat, screenplay), 14–15, 16
Gide, André, 24
Glass Menagerie, The, 21, 22, 30, 42–43, 46, 49–50, 59
Gogh, Vincent van, 104–5, 114
Graves, Mr., 63
Grey, Allan: and Blanche DuBois, 81–82, 83, 88, 97–98; homosexuality of, 4, 36, 38, 45, 65; suicide of, 28, 37, 45, 52, 64, 66, 80, 81–82, 97–98, 99

Group Theatre, 8
Guthke, Karl S., 97

Hairy Ape, The (O'Neill), 8, 9
Heilman, Robert, 88
Hellman, Lillian, 41
Hubbell, Eunice and Steve, 28, 66, 91, 95
Huntleigh, Shep, 39, 64, 81, 82

Idea of a Theater, The (Fergusson), 22
Immoralist, The (Gide), 31
I Rise in Flame, Cried the Phoenix, 45
Irony and Drama (States), 83, 88–89

Jackson, Esther Merle, 108
Jailhouse Rock (Trosper and Young, screenplay and story), 14
Jokes and Their Relation to the Unconscious (Freud), 115
Joyce, James, 2
Julius Caesar (Mankiewicz, script), 13
Jung, Carl, 23

Kaufmann, Walter, 23
Kazan, Elia, 9, 12, 50, 52, 56, 58, 101, 112
Kernan, Alvin B., 113, 117
Kingsley, Sidney, 41
Kowalski, Stanley: ambiguity of, 9, 57; and Blanche DuBois, 17–18, 25, 26, 35, 45, 47, 50–51, 54, 56–58, 59–60, 69–70, 79, 81, 83, 84–86, 89, 90–91, 94, 95, 116; Brando and Quinn's portrayal of, 8, 9, 10, 58, 89; clothing of, 51, 55; dishonesty of, 38–39, 80, 91; earthiness of, 52–53, 57; and Harold Mitchell, 70, 73, 89–90, 97, 101; insensitivity of, 4, 9, 10, 30, 45, 47, 59, 66, 69, 79, 80, 89–90, 94; intimacy's importance to, 89, 90–91; as realist, 17, 18; sensitivity of, 38–39, 59, 90; sensuality and sexuality of, 16, 24, 25, 45, 47, 57, 59, 74, 81, 96; and Stella Kowalski, 26, 27, 28, 29, 37, 39, 47, 57, 60, 70, 85, 86, 87, 88, 89–90, 91, 94–95, 101, 120; vitality of, 10, 28, 56–57, 96

Kowalski, Stella: and Blanche DuBois, 27–28, 37, 82, 84, 85, 87, 88, 89, 90, 116; general characteristics of, 19, 29, 47, 66, 92, 120; and Stanley Kowalski, 26, 27, 28, 29, 37, 39, 47, 57, 60, 70, 85, 86, 87, 88, 89–90, 91, 94–95, 101, 120; weakness of role of, 30–31, 47
Krause, David, 94
Krutch, Joseph Wood, 49, 86, 90

Lady Chatterley's Lover (Lawrence), 44, 47
Lady of Larkspur Lotion, The, 46
Langer, Susanne, 98
Lawrence, D. H., 2, 4, 9, 44–45
Lévi-Strauss, Claude, 117
Lewis, Sinclair, 41
Life of the Drama (Bentley), 94

McCarthy, Mary, 66
Mannoni, O., 112, 113–14, 115
Memoirs, 4, 5, 6, 103
Men, The (Foreman, screenplay and story), 13
Meilziner, Jo, 50
Milk Train Doesn't Stop Here Anymore, The, 46
Miller, Arthur, 33, 35, 41–42, 47
Miller, Jordan Y., 79
Mr. Graves. See Graves, Mr.
Mitch. See Mitchell, Harold
Mitchell, Harold (Mitch): and Blanche DuBois, 28, 37–38, 39, 40, 45, 66–67, 83, 88, 90, 91, 97, 116, 118; general characteristics of, 37–38, 71, 92, 97; and Stanley Kowalski, 70, 73, 89–90, 97, 101
"Modernism" in Modern Drama (Krutch), 90
Modern Tragicomedy (Guthke), 97
Mummers, The, 41, 42

Nelson, Benjamin, 57
Nietzsche, Friedrich, 21, 23, 24–25, 30, 95–96
Night Café (Gogh), 26–27, 51, 104–5
Night of the Iguana, The, 3, 44
Nurse (in Streetcar Named Desire), 74–75

Odets, Clifford, 8, 9, 41
O'Neill, Eugene, 11, 41
On the Waterfront (Schulberg, screenplay and story), 13
Orpheus Descending, 42

Pinter, Harold, 53
Pirandello, Luigi, 17, 19
Play and Its Parts, A (Weales), 51
Poker Night, The. See Streetcar Named Desire, A
Presley, Elvis, 15–16

Quinn, Anthony, 10

Rebel Without a Cause (Ray and Stern, screenplay and story), 13–14, 15
Rimbaud, Arthur, 5–6
Rose Tattoo, The, 21

Sean O'Casey (Krause), 94
Shakespeare, William, 53
Shaw, Irwin, 58
Shep. See Huntleigh, Shep
Sontag, Susan, 77
Stanislavsky, Konstantin, 8, 12
Stanley. See Kowalski, Stanley
States, Bert O., 83, 88–89
Steinbeck, John, 8
Stella. See Kowalski, Stella (in Streetcar Named Desire)
Steve. See Hubbell, Eunice and Steve
Streetcar Named Desire, A: ambiguity in, 93, 94, 95, 98; Apollonian-Dionysian motif in, 21, 23, 24, 25, 26, 28, 29–30, 96; art vs. nature in, 114, 119; audience's and readers' roles in, 58, 59, 66, 87, 96, 99, 113, 114–15, 116, 117, 119–20, 121; autobiographical elements in, 77; baby's role in, 109; Belle Reve's role in, 36, 50, 56, 65, 66, 67, 69; birthday celebration in, 53, 64; body vs. soul in, 9, 23, 26, 61, 69, 76, 120; chaos vs. order in, 46, 75; chorus's role in, 118–19, 121; colors in, 103–7, 108, 109; as conflict between protagonists, 9, 10, 17–18, 24, 57, 59, 62,

Streetcar Named Desire, A (continued)
68, 80, 90, 98, 105, 116–18; costuming in, 50–51, 59; death in, 61, 64–65, 76, 100, 108–9, 116, 121; Elysian Fields' role in, 24, 65, 66, 67, 69, 114–15; epigraph to, 3, 6, 24, 47, 63–64, 113, 116; games of chance in, 62, 63, 70–74; general themes in, 38–39, 45–46, 59, 103, 118; *Glass Menagerie* compared to, 21, 30, 59; hysteria in, 113, 115; as interchange of actor, audience, and director, 113, 121; irony in, 4–5, 33–34, 38, 65, 80, 89, 120; light in, 18, 50–51, 53–54, 59, 70, 108, 119; as major work, 3, 49, 60, 93; music and sound in, 26, 52, 53, 55, 56, 59, 66, 68, 114, 119; myth in, 61, 65, 69, 70, 71, 72, 99, 114–15; names in, 63, 64, 65, 66, 71, 73, 77, 106; paintings in, 103, 104; psychological motifs in, 24, 25, 30, 94; rape scene in, 18–19, 26, 29, 30, 52, 55–56, 58, 62, 69, 79, 80–81, 95; realism and reality in, 18–19, 24, 29, 31, 49–50, 55, 56, 58, 59, 60, 100, 101, 113, 114–15, 121; scrim in, 50, 55, 59, 116, 119; semiotic interpretation of, 117–18; sensitive individual vs. society in, 43, 45, 57, 86, 98–99; setting of, 24, 50, 104, 113, 116, 119; sexual imagery in, 67, 76; as social protest, 21, 94; structure of, 28–29, 49, 62, 91, 92, 93; style of, 3, 4–5, 21, 26–27, 44, 76–77, 91–92; symbolism in, 24, 26, 29, 30, 31, 49, 61–63, 71, 100, 114–15; title of, 62, 104; as tragedy, 10, 33, 77, 80, 91, 93, 96; as tragicomedy, 93–94, 96–97, 98, 101; violence in, 25–26, 105; voyages in, 63, 64, 70, 73, 74, 100–101; water imagery in, 50, 73, 74, weaknesses of, 3, 6, 21, 23–24, 30–31, 93, 96–97, 108. *See also specific characters*
Street vendor, 52
Suddenly Last Summer, 2, 21, 29, 42, 46

Summer and Smoke: Alma Winemiller's role in, 42, 43, 44, 45, 46; general themes in, 43, 59, 60, 103; John Buchanan's role in, 44, 47
Sweet Bird of Youth, 42
Sypher, Wylie, 98

Taylor, Henry, 59
"Temptation of [Saint] Flaubert, The" (Valéry), 76
Tennessee Williams (Falk), 85, 86
Theatre in Our Time, The (Gassner), 96
"Timeless World of a Play, The," 22
Tischler, Nancy, 79
Tragedy and Melodrama (Heilman), 88
Triumph of Life (Shelley), 3
Tynan, Kenneth, 3, 4

"Ulalume" (Poe), 64

Valéry, Paul, 76
Viva Zapata! (Steinbeck, screenplay and story), 13

Weales, Gerald, 51
"When Lilacs Last in the Dooryard Bloom'd" (Whitman), 3
Whitman, Walt, 4
Wilder, Thornton, 2
Wild One, The (Paxton, screenplay), 13
Williams, Thomas Lanier (Tennessee): awards received by, 41, 44; background of, 41–42; decline of, 2, 3; literary influences on, 2–3, 4, 9, 21, 23, 24–25, 30, 44–45, 70–71, 75, 77, 104, 105, 114; as writer, 2, 19, 41–42, 47, 101
Williams's plays: characterization in, 17, 29; controversial nature of, 41; general themes in, 42, 77; realism and reality in, 17, 19, 22; symbolism in, 17, 19, 21, 22, 44, 77; weaknesses of, 21, 44 *See also specific works*